organic and chic

organic and chic

CAKES, COOKIES, AND OTHER SWEETS
THAT TASTE AS GOOD AS THEY LOOK

sarah magid

With photographs by Noah Sheldon

WILLIAM MORROW

An Imprint of HarperCollins*Publishers*

Illustrations © 2009 by Sarah Magid
Child drawings © 2009 by Clyde Dwyer
Photographs © 2009 by Noah Sheldon
Additional photo credits: Matthew Tapper, page 161; Lesley
Unruh, page 4 (above left), page 7 (bottom left), 191 (above left), 209,
234 (bottom right), 244, 245; pages v, 7, 131, 135, and 192 from the
author's collection.

HarperCollins books may be purchased for educational, business, or
sales promotional use. For information, please write: Special Markets
Department, HarperCollins Publishers, 10 East 53rd Street, New York,
NY 10022.

FIRST EDITION

Designed by Judith Stagnitto Abbate / Abbate Design

Library of Congress Cataloging-in-Publication Data

Magid, Sarah.
    Organic and chic: cakes, cookies, and other sweets that taste as good as
they look / Sarah Magid; with photographs by Noah Sheldon.—1st ed.
        p. cm.
    Includes index.
    ISBN 978-0-06-167358-0
1. Desserts.   2. Cake.   3. Cookies.   4. Cookery
(Natural foods)   I. Title.
    TX773.M2343 2009
    641.8'6—dc22   2008031741

09   10   11   12   13   ID/PX   10 9 8 7 6 5 4 3 2 1

contents

introduction

WHEN MY THREE-YEAR-OLD SON, Clyde, asked me to buy him a box of Twinkies at the grocery store one day, I quickly told him that we would go home and bake better ones ourselves. My parents never allowed me to eat this kind of food as a child, and after one glance at the bewildering ingredients (polysorbate 60, anyone?) listed on the package, I decided they probably knew what they were doing. So in order to avoid a DEFCON 3 meltdown, my son and I whipped up our own version: dark-chocolate sponge cake with a vanilla-cream filling, using all organic ingredients—and the popular "Goldie" was born (see page 137).

This experience, and its yummy, healthy, and happy outcome, inspired me to start thinking about other kinds of "forbidden" sweets and how I could re-create them with entirely organic ingredients. The results were spectacular: treats tasting far better than the original, and without ingredients that sound more like gasoline additives than food. That month, Clyde and I experimented with all kinds of "junk food gone good," and now his eyes rarely glance at the junk-food aisle.

Although my love of cupcakes and everyday delicious sweets means that I'm not your typical health nut, as a mother I do consider myself a part of the organic lifestyle, a term I use to describe the growing number of people who are choosing to buy and eat local, organic, and fair-trade foods. I use organic ingredients for a few reasons: Most important, they're better for you, and they taste better, too. For baking in particular, it's always helpful to remember that organic dairy products contain none of the hormones or antibiotics that conventional dairy products do. Similarly, organic fruit, which makes delicious cake toppings and fillings, is not only free of pesticides but also has been shown to contain both more nutrients and more flavor. And eating organic is better for the environment, because certified organic farms have strict guidelines about how the soil is treated and how the water runoff is managed. (For example, one organic sugar plant in Florida turns its excess energy into reusable energy for running its refinery mills, as well as generating power for 40,000 homes!) Now that eating organic has become more mainstream, we have the choice of buying and using organic ingredients in a modern, fresh way, shaking off that old crusty health-food-store stigma.

My style of baking reflects this new way of using organic ingredients, seasonal fruits, and healthful alternatives in simple, delectable sweets and fabulous, fancy cakes. My obsession with sweets and cakes, however, began before I became knowledgeable about the benefits of eating organic and before I became a mother. The obsession started nearly a decade ago, when I was designing shoes for Tommy Hilfiger. At a party for a coworker who had a fierce love of all things cats, I baked a "kitty litter birthday cake," which I served in a real litter pan and scooped with a real scooper (all bought new, I assure you). I crushed vanilla cookies and dyed them pale blue and green to simulate litter and scattered the litter with my Chocolate Plastic Dough (page 202) rolled into catlike perfection. The confused looks and loud laughter of my colleagues diminished when they tasted the moist homemade cake underneath. All told, the cake was a smashing success.

I began to bake all kinds of experimental desserts in my off-hours, while I continued working in the fashion world during the day. After a few years, my cakes became more sophisticated and refined, and my increasing awareness of healthy eating and the environment led me to use exclusively organic ingredients. Although I still worked full-time in fashion, I no longer baked on a whim. I began taking classes with master cake decorators at the Institute of Culinary Education in New York City, and before long

I developed my signature style: cakes with beautiful—if slightly quirky—decorations made, of course, with all organic ingredients.

With the birth of my two children, Clyde and Ruby, I decided that it was time to prioritize my love of all things sweet. I had been designing shoes and jewelry for almost ten years, and I traveled often to shoe factories in Taiwan, jewelry factories in China, and trade shows in Hong Kong. I longed for a life that could somehow balance my love of fashion and design with my love of family and food. As I began more actively applying my creative skills to quality organic baking—a unique niche in the cake design world—I drew attention from like-minded people who care about the quality of their ingredients but also cherish beautiful, inventive cakes. These people share my love of nature and beauty—of wanting the world to sparkle.

As my baking business developed, my client base broadened, and as my children began to grow, I noticed how many moms and dads were equally interested in feeding their families in a healthy, fun way. It made me reflect on my childhood, and on the interest my mom took in feeding her family.

I grew up in a small beach community in Southern California, where health food reigned and backyards were overgrown with fruit trees and bushes dripping with figs, oranges, roses, and lemons, and with wild strawberry patches. Our meals featured traditional Jewish food (greasy and yummy), as well as tofu pizza that didn't look or taste much different than cardboard. We used the fruit and flowers from our backyard to make jams and pies for each holiday, party, and birthday, and we spent joyful time together, much of it centering around food. My mom loved to make a mess in the kitchen, and I have many memories of standing next to her, beating egg whites in a special bowl for what seemed like a million Passover cakes. At the time, we had only a hand mixer, so my arm would ache for days, but

I'm reminded of the conversation and laughter we shared over the whipped whites each time I bake with my own kids. My mom got wild when she baked, with flour and sugar spilling everywhere, but that process taught me so much: baking is fun, it can be messy, and it's not just about the finished product—but if that product is beautiful and tastes great, so much the better. The cakes my mother baked for our family are the same ones that I bake for my son and daughter. And though some classics are meant to stay unchanged, I would not be my mother's daughter if I did not "improve" upon them by using all organic ingredients.

My two children provide me with laughter from the deepest part of my soul and the inspiration to do the things that make me happy. Clyde, who is almost five now, loves to bake with me. He has a train-theme apron, a race-car rubber spatula, a red whisk, and a coordinated bandana to cover his hair (as an accessories designer, I'm quite tickled by his love of coordination and color). "Children's Goodies" (page 189) includes our favorite recipes that we bake together, ones that range from easy—for an after-school treat—to more time-consuming for rainy days.

Ruby, who just turned one, is the kitchen musician and baking muse. Too young to measure flour in a mixing cup, she bangs the cups on the stainless-steel mixing bowls and gnaws on rubber spatulas. She smiles and cheers me on in her baby babble as I mix, whisk, and pour batter into pans. It's important for me to teach my children about the origins of food, how it's important to feed your body right, and what exactly goes into a recipe—of course, all in a way that a child can comprehend.

· · ·

Wearing clip-ons for my third birthday

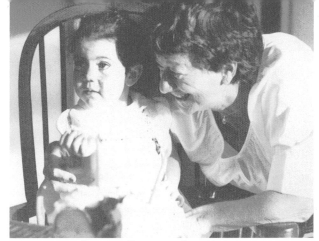

Grandma Eva at my first birthday

My mom's first birthday

Clyde's first birthday—born on 7/11, his party included a
slurpee-shaped cake

Ruby's first birthday—a tea party

A pink cake for my fifth birthday

TODAY WE HAVE THE CHOICE of eating organic. I like supporting small farms that are trying to make a positive impact on our environment, and I stay up-to-date on how organic food has positive benefits for our bodies and for our world. I also love meeting farmers at local farmers' markets and buying their freshly picked vegetables and fruit. These choices foster a more natural connection to what goes into our bodies, and to how humans once ate; it's how nature intended our food cycle to be. Nevertheless, sometimes finding a certain organic ingredient is a pain, particularly if you live far from a city. Sometimes my local shop will run out of organic chocolate when I'm making a cake, so I've had to use a good-quality non-organic variety instead. Above all, I believe that baking should be fun. Sometimes that means that you have to be flexible when it comes to which ingredients you use. I wouldn't want anyone not to bake simply because they didn't have the correct organic ingredients on hand. But because I think the organic ingredients make each recipe taste better and are better for you, I emphasize them in this book.

In *Organic and Chic,* you'll learn how to use organic ingredients to make stylish and delicious party cakes and cookies. The recipes range from my popular Vanilla-Bean Butter Cake (page 37) to my notorious Goldies (page 137), with lots of beautiful pictures and tips to help you along the way. It's time to shake off the notion that organic cuisine is something out of a health-food store from the seventies! I hope the pages that follow will inspire you to develop your own personal style so you can dazzle friends and family.

The experience of baking can create more than just fabulous-looking and great-tasting sweets. When my son and I bake together—even as he spills most of the ingredients out of the bowl—I know that we're not only having fun but also building memories through taste and love. Just as my mom did for me, I hope to pass down the idea that the very process of baking nurtures and sustains people as much as the result does. When I bring one of my sweets into the room—whether at a wedding or an intimate dinner party—the expression on people's faces turns that celebration into a memory I never forget. That's what baking should be. I am thrilled to share with you *Organic and Chic* and its expression of living well, encompassing quality, fashion, style, and, always, family.

> Decorating techniques can be found in detail in "Design Techniques," starting on page 213. Although I've suggested my favorite fillings and frostings for each recipe, feel free to mix and match to come up with your own unique creations. Most important, have fun, make a big mess, and enjoy every bite!

guide to organic
ingredients

FLOUR

Using organic flour is important, particularly when considering how much flour goes into baking a cake or cookies. In addition to being bleached and bromated, commercial flour may come from wheat that's been sprayed with some combination of synthetic fertilizers, herbicides, pesticides, and fumigants. When you buy organic flour, you can be assured that none of these is being used on the grain.

In many of my recipes, I try to include some whole wheat pastry flour, which is finely ground whole wheat with a lower gluten content than standard whole wheat flour, so it can be used in delicate recipes. Because the outer bran of the wheat is included, the flour contains more fiber, nutrients, and vitamins. However, in some recipes, you must use white flour or else the cake will be gummy and heavy.

When you measure out flour, never pack it into the measuring cup, or you'll be using more than the recipe calls for. (It's just like brown sugar: when you pack it into the cup, you're actually putting more in.) I gently scoop the flour out of the bag with the measuring cup and then slide a knife across the top to level it. I like to place a large sifter on top of the bowl, so that I can sift all the dry ingredients at once. I use smaller sifters with a standing mixer—when I need to sift powdered sugar for frosting, for example.

King Arthur Flour   I prefer this brand because it offers a range of organic baking flours, and the quality is consistent. One of the largest flour companies in the United States, King Arthur is 100 percent employee owned and contributes to the local community, making donations to hurricane-ravaged areas and food shelters. My favorite flour is the Organic Artisan Bakers flour, which I use in all my cakes. Check out the King Arthur Web site for interesting organic bread mixes and nerdy baking Q&A's. www.kingarthurflour.com

Arrowhead Mills   I love their whole wheat pastry flour, which is finely ground with more nutrients than classic all-purpose flour. It has a lower gluten content than standard whole wheat flour, which means it provides a finer texture and a lighter consistency for cakes and cookies. This company also sells all kinds of alternative flours, such as spelt, barley, and oat, which I use for baking experiments. www.arrowheadmills.com

SUGAR

Most commercial white sugars are made from sugar beets, not sugarcane. Sugar beets are cheaper, as they can grow in various weather conditions and require only one form of processing to turn them into sugar. Although the two types of sugar may look similar, they can act differently in baking. A 1999 article in the *San Francisco Chronicle* described a taste test of beet sugar versus cane sugar, and the results favored cane sugar's subtler, more even taste. Some bakers the paper interviewed said that the beet sugar acted differently when they made caramel apples or even crème brûlée.

The process of refining is also different for organic sugar. According to the *Vegetarian Journal,* animal-bone charcoal is commonly used in processing conventional sugar to create "white" sugar. (Hain Celestial Company and Whole Foods mark their powdered sugar "Vegan Powdered Sugar" to inform consumers that their sugar is processed differently.) Organic sugars don't use this process, and most cane sugar is a light brown color because it's closer to its natural state.

Sugar that is grown without herbicides, chemicals, and pesticides and isn't overly processed is better for you. Most of my recipes call for organic cane sugar, a versatile light brown-colored sugar that has a mellow sweetness. There are other types of cane sugar, such as Rapadura, which retains some of the nutrients from the sugarcane. It has a deeper, more molasses-like flavor, so I like to use it in recipes that can stand up to it—such as the Crispy, Chewy Oatmeal Raisin Cookies (page 109). Other alternatives to sugar are muscovado (a form of unrefined cane sugar) and maple sugar (dried maple syrup that has been ground to a sugar consistency). These have more assertive flavors than cane sugar, and I find they work best with fruit, such as in Freyja's Strawberry-Rhubarb Pie (page 182) or in Colombe's Wheat-Free Lavender Apricot Crisp (page 185).

Organic sugar will never contain any product that is considered a genetically modified organism (GMO), the term for food that has had its DNA altered to give the plant new traits. For example, the seeds of a genetically modified tomato or sugar beet have been changed to be heartier and resistant to certain insects, bacteria, and/or weather conditions. This allows for a more consistent product and yields more fruit, but it has not been studied long-term to see if it's a safe farming practice or what type of effects it has on humans. Many conventional sugar-beet farmers use genetically modified sugar beets, but it's a highly controversial issue, and many argue that science should not tamper with Mother Nature. Also, most conventional corn is genetically modified, so it's important to buy organic cornstarch, corn syrup, and other corn-derived products.

Florida Crystals   This is the first company to make organic sugar, and their products are pesticide- and herbicide-free and grown without chemical fertilizers. The company works harmoniously with its marshlike environment, using owls and wading birds to ward off rodents! But most impressive is its onsite renewable-energy power plant, which extracts energy from the excess sugarcane stalks to power the sugar mills, refinery operations, and 40,000 homes. This is just one example of how organic farming can improve our environment.
www.floridacrystals.com

Wholesome Sweeteners   This company tries to work with fair trade–certified farm cooperatives whenever possible, which means the small farms are paid fairly and directly. This helps support families, farmers, and the local community. The company also recycles fuel to generate electricity for its mill and nearby villages. Its sugar is organic and hand-cultivated. You can even go on the Web site to find the farm that sourced your sweetener. I use their products frequently and like the taste of their powdered sugar, which doesn't have the chalky flavor that most conventional brands do.

www.wholesomesweetners.com

Hain Celestial Company This company makes organic sugar and many other products. I've used their dark-brown sugar and love it. Because it is a large company, this brand is more commonly found at nationwide supermarket chains. Some of their better-known brands are Arrowhead Mills, Health Valley, and Earth's Best, among others.

www.hain-celestial.com

Private—Label Brands It's amazing to me how many private-label organic brands are now found in large and specialty grocery stores, including giants such as Costco and Wal-Mart. Because I live near a Whole Foods, I stock up on their private 365 label sugar, powdered sugar, and organic chocolate chips. I find the quality excellent, and the products make great baked goods. When I visit my relatives in Chicago, I buy *O* Organics at the local Dominick's chain. Private-label organic brands means that the prices are lower and the products are accessible to more people. Hooray!

Look for these private-label brands that sell organic products—be sure to check the label!

365 (at Whole Foods)
O Organics (at Dominick's)
Archer Farms (at Target)
Parent's Choice (at Wal-Mart)
Safeway Select (at Safeway)
Kirkland Signature (at Costco)

DAIRY PRODUCTS

Organic dairy products contain no antibiotics or added growth hormones, and the cows, hens, and goats eat pesticide-free feed. Organic feed doesn't contain products from genetically modified sources. When livestock eat conventional grain or feed, the insecticides, growth hormones, fungicides, and pesticides consolidate as toxins in the fat of the animals, which passes into the milk and butter we eat. Even if we're exposed to only trace amounts, toxins can build up over time.

MILK

Because scientists still do not know the impact on our health, at a minimum, avoid drinking milk that contains the growth hormone rBGH (a bovine growth hormone), which is already banned in Europe. The Centers for Disease Control speculate that the increased use of antibiotics in livestock is affecting human antibiotic resistance, and that the antibiotics are passed to consumers at higher levels than once thought. One of the leading researchers in the study, Edward Belongia, M.D., said, "We need to have drugs to treat sick animals," adding, "but we should not be using antibiotics to promote growth."

Studies have shown that organic milk contains higher levels of vitamin E, omega-3 fatty acids, and antioxidants than conventional milk. A study by the University of Wisconsin, published in the *British Journal of Nutrition*, showed that the higher nutritional value of organic milk can be credited to the open pastures most organic cows are allowed to graze in, as compared to the confined lots or feeding pens found on many conventional dairy farms. The strict organic guidelines set by the USDA also affect the way the cows are treated. For example, when a cow on an organic farm becomes sick, it receives conventional antibiotics but is removed from the milking herd permanently, unlike conventional milking cows. I may be a city girl, but I imagine cows are much happier when they are free to munch on grass—and I think it makes for a better product.

Organic milk also tends to reflect the change in seasons: the milk that I buy from my farmers' market tastes more grassy in the summertime and more buttery in the winter. It may be a subtle difference, but I imagine it's probably how milk tasted when it was delivered fresh to your doorstep decades ago.

BUTTER

Butter is concentrated milk fat, so any of the hormones or pesticides contained in the milk increase when it is made into butter. The Pesticide Action Network of North America ranks nonorganic butter as the food most contaminated with persistent organic pollutants (POPs), some of the most dangerous toxic chemicals. Because of this, organic butter should always be used in baking and eating. Like organic milk, it's free of pesticides, antibiotics, and growth hormones, and its taste is rich and truly buttery. Eating organic butter greatly reduces the amount of toxins we ingest, particularly important for children's small, developing bodies.

The following brands stand out for their pledge to support smaller organic farms, their fantastic educational and outreach programs, and their expanding product lines for kids. As a mom, I think it's great to see more healthful organic snacks, yogurts, and other products for kids!

Horizon Organic   This company offers a wide range of organic dairy products, including food kids like, such as yogurt sticks and string cheeses. My son, Clyde, recognized their flying cow logo at age two and thinks it's superhero-cow milk. Horizon Organic supports more than 550 small organic farms, offers great recipes on its Web site, and is expanding its products to include ice cream and eggnog.
www.horizonorganic.com

Organic Valley Farms   This farm collective has been around for over twenty years and now employs more than 1,200 farms to make a range of organic products, from delicious dairy to meat and produce. Their Web site is regularly updated with news regarding organic foods, recipes, and events, such as a country fair at their headquarters in Wisconsin. The "Reading Room" page contains links to relevant articles, blogs, and facts about eating organic, organic farming, and organic news.
www.organicvalley.coop

Stonyfield Farm   One of the most commendable things about this company is how they are transforming food options in the nation's public school system, including swapping in healthier food selections in vending machines. Their site contains valuable tips for healthful cooking and information on organic farming and the ways the company is supporting the environment.
www.stonyfieldfarm.com

Ronnybrook   Local to the New York region, this farm's milk can be found in farmers' markets. The farm is known for its creamy, delicious yogurt drinks and expanding line of yogurts, cheeses, ice

creams, and eggs. Its milk products are non-homogenized, meaning that the cream is allowed to separate from the milk (typically, cream is processed to be evenly distributed in the milk, for a uniform texture). Non-homogenized milk is creamier, has a richer flavor, and needs to be shaken a bit before you pour it. And Ronnybrook ice creams are incredibly buttery and delicious! Ronnybrook also sells its milk in great recycled-glass bottles (sometimes I use them as vases instead of returning them to the market).
www.ronnybrook.com

Natural by Nature   This company sells non-homogenized milk from grass-fed cows and pasteurizes it at lower temperatures to preserve flavor and nutrition. Natural by Nature also makes a fantastic whipped cream in a can.
www.natural-by-nature.com

Woodstock Farms   This company makes my favorite organic butter, and I like their simple philosophy and consistent taste and quality. They offer a wide range of products from snacks to pickles; it seems as though every time I visit my local store, they are offering more alternative organic products.
www.woodstock-farms.com

Hawthorne Valley Farm   This upstate New York farm, one of the first to be certified organic in the United States, sells the best fresh buttermilk, which I use in my baking, at Greenmarkets in New York City. Their farm is open to the public for visiting or buying milk fresh from the cows. They even have internships and a school onsite, which I fantasize about sending my kids to so I can milk cows all day long.
www.hawthornevalleyfarm.org

EGGS

Organic chickens are raised according to strict guidelines, ensuring that they eat organic feed and have access to the outdoors and a cage-free environment. Organic eggs often contain a brighter yolk and have a creamier texture. Some organic chicken farms add omega-3 or flaxseed to the chickens' diet to increase the nutritional benefits in the egg fat. Most organic dairy farmers also sell delicious organic eggs: Organic Valley and Ronnybrook (my local favorite from the farmers' market) are two examples. Pete & Gerry's sells tasty eggs too.
www.peteandgerrys.com

OTHER INGREDIENTS

Cacao Nibs   Cacao nibs are crushed bits of cacao beans—which are actually not beans at all, but seeds from the Theobroma plant. Most often, these beans are dried or roasted and then extracted to make cocoa butter for chocolate, or ground into powder to make cocoa powder. Cacao nibs are crushed cacao beans that have not been made into chocolate or cocoa powder. You can find them raw or roasted, and they resemble espresso beans in texture and crunch. They contain no added sugar, so they're bittersweet. They add great texture to cookies—I even use them as a topping for ice cream. They can be found at most specialty and health-food stores or online. Make sure you buy the finely ground variety.

Cocoa Powder   Rapunzel is my favorite brand of organic cocoa powder. It's made from cacao that is grown in farming cooperatives in the Dominican Republic and Bolivia. I like the way it gives my cakes and cookies a rich, dark chocolaty taste. You can find this brand at most specialty stores or online. www.rapunzel.com

Chocolate　　While many organic brands of chocolate are coming into the market, my personal favorite is Green & Black's 70 percent baking chocolate. Even though it's labeled a baking chocolate, it's edible without adding sugar or other sweeteners and has a dark mocha flavor. I also like Rapunzel's 70 percent baking chocolate, which comes in small chocolate disks around an inch in diameter. These super-chic disks are an elegant alternative to the standard chocolate chips in chocolate chip cookies. Like Green & Black's, Rapunzel's is dark, rich, and bittersweet. If you prefer a sweeter ganache, you can always use semisweet chocolate instead of bittersweet. Look for these brands in specialty food stores or online. www.greenandblack.com

Peanut Butter　　Clyde likes to push the button on the fresh organic peanut butter grinder in our local grocery store. In natural peanut butter like this, the oils separate and can cause uneven results in baking. For that reason I prefer to use a blended peanut butter such as Whole Kids from Whole Foods. Because it contains organic binders, the oil and peanut butter won't separate, keeping it smooth, creamy, and perfect for recipes. Whole Kids peanut butter is organic and inexpensive.

Shortening　　Organic shortening contains no trans fats, hydrogenated oils, or artificial preservatives. The only brand to look for is Spectrum, which makes a wide variety of organic oils for baking and cooking; they can be found at most specialty and health food stores or online.

www.spectrumoils.com

Flavored Extracts   Brands such as Simply Organic, Tropical Traditions, Flavorganics, and Frontier manufacture organic vanilla, almond, and peppermint extracts, among others. Although they're higher priced than conventional extracts, they tend to be stronger and more flavorful, as they are natural and contain no artificial ingredients. Most of these products can be found at Whole Foods or Wild Oats.

www.simplyorganic.com

www.flavorganics.com

cakes and cupcakes
to die for

THE CAKES IN THIS CHAPTER are the ones I'm known for—the ones I've baked for years and love making over and over again, for all kinds of occasions. The recipes can make either cakes or cupcakes, so depending on your mood or the type of party, you can decide which to bake. Chocolate always seems to be the most popular for birthdays, but I've included a few different options, which vary from truly decadent to simple and quick.

In general, when you're making a cake for a party, you should try to allow two days to give yourself optimal decorating time. Although you don't want to bake a cake too far in advance, if you do it the day or night before, wrap it well, and refrigerate it, it will taste fresh and allow you ample time to decorate. Sometimes the baking can take a lot of time, and it's best to save your energy for decorating. In addition, some frostings work best when they have time to set, and decorating is easier when the frosting is not "wet." For example, if I want a cake for Saturday night, I will bake the cake Friday afternoon and, once it's cooled, wrap it well and refrigerate it. Then on Saturday morning I will cut the cake into layers, make the filling, and refrigerate the filled cake while I make the outer frosting. Chilling in between steps also ensures that the cake has a good foundation for the frosting.

golden rules and tips for cakes and cupcakes

IT'S HELPFUL TO SET OUT all your ingredients and measure them before baking. You don't want to be in the middle of the recipe and realize that your milk is spoiled or that you're out of sugar!

MAKE SURE THE OVEN HAS been preheated to the correct temperature.

TO PREVENT YOUR CAKES FROM sticking, always butter or spray your pans, then sprinkle a pinch of flour over them to coat the sides and bottom. (For chocolate cakes, you can substitute cocoa powder for the flour.) I trace the bottom of the pan on a sheet of parchment paper, cut it out, and place the paper in the bottom of the pan. The cakes will slide right out of the pan once they've cooled.

REUSE BUTTER WRAPPERS for the bottoms of small cake pans, instead of parchment paper. I fold the wrapper in half, then in half again, and cut the corners off in a rounded shape. That way when I open it up, it's circular and will fit inside a small pan. It makes me feel very eco-chic too!

IF YOU DON'T HAVE ANY butter left, you can use spray oil and then coat the pan with flour. Although it will not impart that nice butter flavor, it's more important to avoid having your cake stick to the pan.

USE CUPCAKE LINERS TO prevent sticking.

WHEN BEATING EGG WHITES, IT'S best to prepare your mixer and beaters by wiping them down with a mixture of 1 tablespoon organic white vinegar and 1 tablespoon salt. Using a paper towel, rub this mixture all over the bowl and beaters to get rid of any greasy residue, which would prevent the egg whites from getting fluffy.

FILL INDIVIDUAL CUPCAKE MOLDS at least two-thirds full to achieve a nice round dome on top.

USE A SMALL TRADITIONAL ICE-CREAM scoop to ensure that each cupcake contains the same amount of batter and bakes evenly. Sometimes I also use a small ladle, to avoid dripping batter on the pan.

NEVER, EVER OPEN THE OVEN door during the first 15 minutes of baking. The cake may deflate if you do so. Its best to check your cakes and cupcakes through the window in the oven door, and to open the oven only to test them a few minutes before they're supposed to be done.

TO CHECK IF YOUR CAKE or cupcake is done, use a cake tester (found at most food supply stores) or a good old-fashioned toothpick. Stick the tester or the toothpick in the center of the cake. Your cake is done when the tester comes out clean, meaning there is no batter or gooey clumps sticking to it. If the cake isn't done but has baked for the prescribed time, continue baking it in 3- to 4-minute increments until the tester comes out clean.

LET CUPCAKES COOL SLIGHTLY in the pan before removing them. If you remove them too quickly, they could become misshapen.

NEVER FROST A WARM CAKE or cupcake! The frosting will melt, disappear into the cracks and crevices of your cake, and not set properly.

chocolate love blossom

This is based on a cake my mom often made. It came from Maida Heatter's Book of Great Chocolate Desserts, *except that Mom could never stick to the recipe. The sour cream tempers the cake's sweetness, and the cake itself is so moist that it almost resembles a pound cake in texture. I fill it with Vanilla Whipped Cream tinted in a bright color or Red Currant Curd, and cover it with Sweet Chocolate Ganache. It's the perfect cake for beginners—my husband found my recipe journal and baked this cake for my birthday!*

6 ounces organic unsweetened chocolate

1 stick ($1/2$ cup) organic unsalted butter

1 cup extremely hot brewed organic fair—trade coffee

2 cups organic all—purpose flour

1 teaspoon baking powder

$1/2$ teaspoon salt

3 organic eggs, separated

1 cup firmly packed organic light—brown sugar

1 cup organic cane sugar

$3/4$ cup organic sour cream

1 tablespoon organic vanilla extract

Vanilla Whipped Cream (page 180) or Red Currant Curd (page 92)

Sweet Chocolate Ganache (recipe follows)

Preheat the oven to 350°F. Butter and flour two 8-inch round cake pans or one 10-inch tube pan, or line muffin pans with liners. Set aside.

Place the chocolate and butter in a small stainless-steel bowl, and pour the hot coffee over them. Cover the bowl with aluminum foil or with the lid of a pot, and set aside until the chocolate is melted, about 5 minutes. Whisk to combine the butter, chocolate, and coffee. Set aside.

In a medium bowl, sift together the flour, baking powder, and salt. Set aside.

In a standing mixer fitted with the paddle attachment, beat the egg yolks on medium speed until they are light in color, 2 to 3 minutes. Reduce the speed to low and add the sugars, beating for 1 minute until combined. Still on low speed, add the chocolate mixture and the sour cream and stir until combined. Then mix in the vanilla.

With the mixer still on low, slowly add the flour mixture in thirds, until just combined. In a clean bowl, beat the egg whites until peaks form. Scoop ½ cup into the batter and mix, then fold in the rest. Pour the batter into the prepared pan(s).

Bake for 40 to 45 minutes, or until a cake tester comes out clean. For cupcakes, bake for about 30 minutes. Cool in the pan(s) on a wire rack for 15 minutes, then unmold and let cool completely.

If you're making a layer cake, place the cooled cakes upside down on cake rounds. Using a serrated knife, slice the cakes in half horizontally and place each layer on a cake round, so that you have four cake layers.

If there's a noticeable dome on the top of any layer, use the serrated knife to gently cut the rounded top off, usually no more than ¼ inch of cake. Eat this yummy bit.

Place ¼ cup of curd or filling onto the center of the cake and, using a small offset spatula, spread it evenly all over the cake to the edge.

To add a layer of cake to the frosted layer, pick up one of the other cake layers on a cake round, bend one edge of the cake round 2 inches away from the cake, and place the exposed corner of cake evenly on top of the frosted layer. With a knife or a clean spatula, slowly remove the layer from the cake round onto the frosted layer, dropping it gently on top.

Repeat by filling and building the remaining layers. Chill before frosting with the ganache.

The first step in frosting is to create a crumb coat, a thin layer of frosting that traps the crumbs before the final coat of frosting is done. Because the cake is chilled, the ganache will harden quickly, so you'll need to be efficient.

When the ganache is warm but not extremely hot, place $1/2$ cup on top of the cake, working quickly with a medium spatula and using a circular motion to spread a thin layer over the top. Place a few table-spoons ganache on a medium offset spatula and frost the sides with a thin layer as well, holding the spatula vertically.

Refrigerate for 15 minutes to set the ganache.

To finish frosting, place another, thicker layer of ganache on top of the crumb coat. If the ganache has hardened slightly, you can always place it on low heat, stirring frequently until it warms up a bit.

sweet chocolate ganache

| MAKES ABOUT 2 CUPS |

1 11.5–ounce package organic semisweet chocolate chips
3.5 ounce dark chocolate (at least 70%) bar, chopped into small pieces

1 stick ($1/2$ cup) organic unsalted butter, cut into pieces
$1/2$ cup organic heavy cream
1 tablespoon organic vanilla extract
$1/2$ teaspoon salt

Combine all the ingredients in a small heavy-bottomed saucepan over low heat and cook, whisking constantly, until the chips and chocolate are just melted. The ganache will thicken as it cools, so you can either pour it warm over cooled cake or cupcakes as a glaze or let it chill slightly for a thicker creamy frosting. The ganache will keep, tightly covered, in the refrigerator for up to 4 days.

| to decorate

To MAKE THE CAKE AS PICTURED ON PAGE 30, bake two batches of cake in 8- and 6-inch pans. It's best to use two of each size for two layers. Extra batter from the 6-inch cake can be used to fill a small tray filled with cupcake liners. Prepare the Love Blossom flowers a few days before (page 226) and the Vanilla Whipped Buttercream (page 84), tinted pale lemon yellow. Use at least three different colors for the flowers, in pink tones—or as I do for baby boy showers, shades of pale blue. Fill, frost, and chill the cakes, then follow the directions to tier the layers on page 242.

The cake is now ready to decorate. Use metallic luster dust to paint vines on the cake, page 238, then use these as the guide to placing the flowers. Place three of the larger flowers in a cluster in the top corner of the cake. Dab some frosting on the back of a small flower and place it inside the center of each larger flower. This will create dimension and texture. Paint the centers with gold metallic luster dust paint.

Continue applying the flowers in a flowing pattern, starting from the top and moving diagonally down the front of the cake, with a few small flowers applied with frosting. Once the flowers are secured on the cake, use the smaller piping tips, such as size 0, 1, or 2, to pipe stamens inside each flower. I like to vary the piped stamens, adding one large dot of frosting in the center of some flowers, a small circle of three or four dots in others, or a circle of small dots with a dot in the center. The different stamen centers give the flowers a whimsical look.

So versatile, this cake can be dressed up
in bright—colored frostings for any party.

vanilla-bean butter cake

This cake is my food version of the LBD (little black dress)—always appropriate to bake and easy to dress up. Fresh-scraped vanilla seeds give the cake a vanilla flavor that the extract alone can't match. My mom baked this cake for all our birthdays, and I continue to bake it for my kids, too. (It makes fabulous mini cupcakes for kids' parties.) It's also a perfect complement to ripe summer fruit, as it is sweet, buttery, and quick to make on a hot day.

2 sticks (1 cup) organic unsalted butter, softened

1 3/4 cups organic cane sugar

4 organic eggs

1 cup organic whole milk

1 tablespoon organic vanilla extract

1/2 organic vanilla bean, seeds scraped out and reserved (see Note)

2 3/4 cups organic all-purpose flour

1 1/2 teaspoons baking powder

1/2 teaspoon salt

Preheat the oven to 350°F. Butter and flour two 8-inch round cake pans, or place liners in muffin pans for 24 cupcakes. Set aside.

In a standing mixer or using a hand mixer, cream the butter and sugar on medium speed for 3 to 5 minutes, until light and fluffy. Scrape the sides of the bowl with a rubber spatula to make sure everything is incorporated. Add the eggs, one at a time, on low speed until incorporated.

In a small bowl, combine the milk, vanilla extract, and vanilla seeds. Set aside.

Sift the flour, baking powder, and salt together in a medium bowl and set aside.

With the mixer on low speed, alternate adding the flour mixture and the vanilla milk in three batches, starting and ending with the flour. When the mixture is almost combined, turn off the mixer and scrape down the sides and bottom of the bowl. Finish mixing the batter by hand with a rubber spatula. Pour the batter into the prepared pans.

Bake for 35 to 40 minutes, or until a touch of pale golden brown appears around the edges and a tester inserted in the center comes out clean. For cupcakes, bake for 25 to 30 minutes.

Let the cakes cool in the pans for 15 minutes. Then invert them onto a wire rack and let them cool completely.

Note: Reserve scraped vanilla pods in a small glass jar with some cane sugar. The pods will infuse the sugar with vanilla, making vanilla sugar, which is great to sprinkle into coffee or onto any baked dessert for an extra vanilla treat.

fillings and frostings |

I like to layer this cake with my Chic Curds (page 92) for summer birthdays, and in the winter fill it with the Sweet Chocolate Ganache (page 33) and frost it in bright colors. The Grapefruit Curd (page 94) tastes particularly good as a filling for a cake frosted with the Classic Americana Icing (page 86). The tartness of the curd is cut by the sweet frosting, making this a perfect mouthful of birthday cake! You can easily tint the Americana Icing bright colors, and because it's a bit stiffer than the Vanilla Whipped Buttercream, you can use it to pipe more delicate details if desired. To prepare the cakes pictured on page 36, tint the frosting bright colors. I make the same flowers as I do for the Chocolate Love Blossom, page 31, except these are all white, and the centers are bright. The cupcakes taste great with these frostings too. Try tinting a range of colors so that a platter of cupcakes looks light and festive.

diablo cake

My husband, Johnny, inspired me to make this cake for his thirtieth birthday. Although he loves my cakes, he wanted something reminiscent of his childhood cakes, which were a combination of Grandma's cakes from scratch and cakes made from a mix. Because it was an important birthday, I wanted to impress the guests, but I also wanted to bake the kind of cake that would make him swoon. After the cake was cut into, all the sophisticates had the same reaction: they loved it, and it reminded most of them of cakes they had when they were little. I was quite thrilled with this Proustian moment, and I continue to bake this cake to win my husband over when I'm eyeing a fancy pair of shoes!

This is my version of a devil's food cake (diablo *is "devil" in Spanish), and sometimes I add 1 teaspoon cinnamon, 1/2 teaspoon cayenne pepper, and a pinch of fresh black pepper to give it a Mexican flair.*

Diablo Cake always tastes great with Mocha Buttercream (page 91) or Sweet Chocolate Ganache (page 33).

1½ cups organic all—purpose flour

1 teaspoon baking powder

2 teaspoons baking soda

½ teaspoon salt

1 cup hot brewed organic fair—trade coffee (see Note)

1 cup organic unsweetened cocoa powder, plus extra for dusting

2 sticks (1 cup) organic unsalted butter, softened

1 cup organic light—brown sugar

1 cup organic cane sugar

3 organic eggs

1 cup organic buttermilk

1 tablespoon organic vanilla extract

Preheat the oven to 350°F. Butter two 8-inch round cake pans and dust them with cocoa powder, or place liners in 2 muffin pans for 24 cupcakes. Set aside.

In a large bowl, sift the together the flour, baking powder, baking soda, and salt. Set aside.

In a small bowl, whisk the hot coffee and cocoa powder together. Set aside.

Using a standing mixer fitted with the paddle attachment, cream the butter on low speed for 1 minute. Then add the sugars and beat on low speed for 3 minutes until light and fluffy.

With the mixer running, add the eggs, one at a time. Then add the buttermilk and vanilla extract until thoroughly combined.

Alternate adding the dry ingredients and the chocolate-coffee mixture, starting and ending with the dry ingredients. When the mixture is almost combined, turn off the mixer and finish mixing by hand (to avoid overbeating). Pour the batter into the prepared pans.

Bake for 35 to 40 minutes, or until a tester inserted in the center comes out clean. Cool in the pans for 10 minutes, then invert onto a wire rack.

Note: I like to use decaf coffee in case pregnant mommies or kids eat some of the cake. Just dissolve 1 tablespoon organic instant decaf in 1 cup hot water.

| *to decorate*

Baby Bird Cake|

TO BAKE THE CAKE AS PICTURED, prepare 4 batches of cake as follows: 2 batches for two 12-inch pans, 1 batch for two 9-inch pans, 1 batch for two 6-inch pans. The filling is 1 batch of Espresso Whipped Buttercream (page 85), and the frosting is 2 1/2 batches of tinted Vanilla Whipped Buttercream (page 84). This cake can be tinted many colors, but I find that Wedgwood blue always looks great with dark brown. See page 228 on how to make the bird's nest and eggs. For the branches, tint excess frosting dark brown. Pipe the frosting with a size 12 tip for the main branches, and then a smaller tip such as a 2 or 4 for the more delicate branches.

easiest chocolate cake

This is the easiest chocolate cake in the world—perhaps in the universe! You don't even need eggs, butter, or milk, and you probably have all the ingredients on hand. I use this recipe when I'm in a time crunch, because nothing needs to be creamed, beaten, or whipped; you literally just stir things together. It tastes like the best dark chocolate sponge cake you have ever eaten. It's also the base for Goldies (page 137) and Silver Ring-a-Dings (page 141).

You really can please all kinds of people with this one. It happens to be vegan, since there are no dairy products in it. That sounds scary to some people, so don't tell them until after they've eaten about three slices!

2 ¼ cups organic all–purpose flour

2 cups organic cane sugar

1 cup organic unsweetened cocoa powder

2 teaspoons baking soda

½ teaspoon salt

1 tablespoon organic vanilla extract

⅔ cup organic canola oil

2 teaspoons organic white vinegar

2 cups cold water

Preheat the oven to 350°F. Butter and flour two 8- or 9-inch round cake pans, or place liners in 2 muffin pans for 24 cupcakes. Set aside.

In a large bowl, sift the dry ingredients together. Set aside.

In a medium bowl, mix the vanilla extract, oil, vinegar, and cold water.

Slowly whisk the wet ingredients into the dry ingredients, being careful not to overmix. The mixture will be quite wet, but this is okay.

Pour the batter into the prepared pans and bake until a tester inserted in the center comes out clean, about 30 minutes. For cupcakes, the baking time is 24 to 26 minutes.

Cool in the pans for 10 minutes, then invert onto a wire rack to cool.

fillings and frostings |

Good filling options are the Espresso Whipped Buttercream (page 85) or, for a tropical twist, the Coconut-Cream Cheese Frosting (page 50). For the frosting, use a buttercream or chocolate ganache.

| *to decorate*

TO MAKE THE CAKES PICTURED ON PAGE 42, tint sugarpaste and cut out flowers with dogwood cutters (the same flowers used in Chocolate Love Blossom, page 226), or to cut out daisies, see page 229. Fill the cakes with the desired filling, and frost with the Sweet Chocolate Ganache, page 33. Chill to set the frosting, then use the excess ganache as glue to attach the flowers to the cake. Pipe the ganache in the centers of flowers, as well as on the rim of the cake. Use gold metallic luster dust paint to cover the stamen and piped dots with a gold sheen.

carrot cake with cream cheese–lemon zest frosting

| MAKES ONE 8–INCH LAYER CAKE OR 24 CUPCAKES |

My son's teachers beg me to make this cake for his snack day at school. It isn't too sweet, and it has a moist, dense texture from the carrots and pineapple. It's also one of my most popular cakes at weddings and parties. When I make it at home, I throw more things into the batter—for example, a handful of pumpkin seeds or toasted pecans if I have them lying around. The beauty of this recipe is that you can increase the spices or omit the nuts, and it will still taste great.

FOR THE CAKE

$1/3$ cup dried shredded organic
    unsweetened coconut

About 1 pound organic farm–fresh carrots,
    peeled and cut into 2–inch lengths
    (3 cups)

1 cup chopped organic pineapple

$1 1/2$ cups organic all–purpose flour

$1/2$ cup organic whole wheat pastry flour

$1 1/2$ cups organic cane sugar

2 teaspoons baking soda

$2 1/4$ teaspoons organic ground cinnamon

Pinch of freshly grated organic nutmeg

1 teaspoon salt

$1/2$ cup dark–brown sugar

$3/4$ cup organic canola oil

1 tablespoon organic vanilla extract

3 organic eggs

Cream Cheese–Lemon Zest Frosting
    (page 90)

**OPTIONAL ADDITIONS (add one or a
    combination of all three)**

$3/4$ cup chopped toasted organic walnuts

$1/2$ cup organic golden raisins, plumped in
    warm water for 20 minutes and drained

$1/2$ tablespoon minced fresh organic ginger

Preheat the oven to 350°F. Butter and flour two 8-inch round cake pans and line the bottoms with parchment paper (to ensure that the cake will not stick), or place liners in 2 muffin pans for 24 cupcakes. Set aside.

Place the dried coconut in a cup of warm water to soften and set it aside for 15 minutes.

Place the carrots in a food processor and pulse on and off for 1 minute. Then add the pineapple and pulse until the carrots are cut into very small pieces and the pineapple is pureed, 1 to 2 minutes.

In a large bowl, sift together the dry ingredients. Add the brown sugar and use a whisk to break up any lumps.

Drain the coconut and place it in a medium bowl. Add the oil, vanilla extract, eggs, and carrot-pineapple mixture, and whisk to combine.

Add the wet ingredients into the dry, mixing with a rubber spatula to incorporate but not overmix. When the batter is almost mixed, stir in the additions, if using. Pour the batter into the prepared pans.

Bake for 55 minutes, or until the tops are a very golden brown and a tester inserted in the center comes out clean. (It may look as if the cake is too well done, but it takes a while to bake because it's so dense.) For cupcakes, the baking time is 35 to 40 minutes.

Let the cakes cool in the pans for 10 minutes. Then invert them onto a wire rack and let them cool completely.

Fill and frost the cake with the Cream Cheese–Lemon Zest Frosting (for added oomph, add $1/2$ tablespoon minced fresh ginger to the frosting).

to decorate | FILL AND FROST THE CAKE with cream cheese frosting and let chill. Tint 1/2 cup frosting lemon yellow, and use the 10 tip to pipe 5 dots in a circle to create simple buttercup flowers. Then combine any remaining yellow frosting with some additional cream cheese frosting and tint it leaf green. I use tip #67, which pipes small fern stems. Pipe the center stamen with cream cheese frosting and chill to set.

Carrot cake is always a great afternoon sweet. For weddings, I bake a small carrot cake for each table.

coco loco

My sister loves coconut cake, so I bake this every year for her birthday. I use three smaller cake pans to get more height for dramatic effect. (I joke that the older she gets, the higher the cake will be!) The coconut milk in the batter makes this cake tender and gives it a subtle flavor. The layers are smothered in rich coconut frosting, which I layer with chopped fresh pineapple to give it a tropical touch.

2 sticks (1 cup) organic unsalted butter, softened

2 cups organic cane sugar

3 cups organic all−purpose flour

2 teaspoons baking powder

$1/2$ teaspoon salt

1 teaspoon organic vanilla extract

2 teaspoons organic almond extract

$1\frac{1}{4}$ cups organic unsweetened coconut milk

7 organic egg whites

Coconut−Cream Cheese Frosting (recipe follows)

Preheat the oven to 350°F. Butter and flour three 6-inch round cake pans or two 8-inch cake pans, or place liners in 2 muffin pans for 24 cupcakes. Set aside.

In a standing mixer fitted with the whisk attachment, cream the butter and sugar on medium speed for 3 minutes, or until light and fluffy.

In a medium bowl, sift the flour, baking powder, and salt together. Set aside.

In a small bowl, mix the vanilla and almond extracts with the coconut milk. Set aside.

With the mixer running on low speed, alternate adding the flour mixture and the coconut mixture to the butter mixture, beginning and ending with the flour.

Using clean beaters and bowl, beat the egg whites until they are almost stiff but not too dry. Stir a spoonful of the egg whites into the batter, and then, in two batches, fold in the remaining egg whites. Gently pour the batter into the prepared pans, evening out the tops with a rubber spatula.

Bake for 30 to 40 minutes, or until a tester inserted in the center comes out clean. Some parts of an oven can be hotter than others, so it's possible one cake will be done a few minutes before another.

Let the cakes cool in the pans for 10 minutes. Then invert them onto a wire rack and leave until completely cooled.

For a three-layer cake: Place the cake layers on cake rounds. Spread $1/4$ cup frosting across the top of one layer, then press $1/3$ cup chopped pineapple evenly into the frosting. Place the second layer on top and add frosting and pineapple as with the first layer. For the final cake layer, frost the top but omit the pineapple.

A Coconut Primer

Coconut milk is the liquid from the inside of the coconut. It contains a high percentage of water, so it's actually similar in consistency to cow's milk. Cream of coconut is a denser, thicker mixture of milk and shredded coconut meat, so it's richer and more flavorful. I like to use cream of coconut for the frosting; its buttery coconut flavor balances well with the subtle coconut cake. The brand "Let's Do . . . Organic" makes a great-tasting cream of coconut.

Chill in the refrigerator for at least 15 minutes, then spread the remaining coconut cream frosting on the sides and top.

Use your fingers to press the coconut all over the frosted cake. You can tint the coconut colors or toast it and leave it natural.

coconut–cream cheese frosting

1 stick (¹⁄₂ cup) organic unsalted butter,
  softened
8 ounces organic cream cheese,
softened

One 8–ounce box organic unsweetened
  cream of coconut
1 tablespoon organic vanilla extract
3 to 4 cups sifted organic powdered sugar

Using a standing or hand mixer, cream the butter and cream cheese together until pale and fluffy, about 5 minutes.

Add the cream of coconut and vanilla, and mix until just combined.

Sift the powdered sugar over the mixture, and mix on low speed until combined. If the frosting seems too soft to spread, chill it in the refrigerator for 10 minutes to thicken.

to decorate |

For a fluffy, girlie explosion, follow the directions for dyeing shredded coconut in the Snowballz recipe (page 151), using a pale pink, fuchsia, or lavender food coloring. For a more unisex and bright, sunny look, tint the coconut with lemon yellow food coloring. Press the coconut into the frosting.

To toast coconut, spread 1 1/2 cups dried coconut in an even layer on a baking sheet and toast it in a preheated 350°F oven for 5 to 7 minutes, or until lightly browned and crunchy. Press the toasted coconut into the frosting. This makes a great contrast to the creamy frosting and fluffy cake.

uncle gravy's apple cake

| MAKES ONE 9-INCH BUNDT CAKE |

My son, Clyde, had a hard time pronouncing my older brother David's name, so he developed the nickname "Uncle Gravy." David is an architect and artist who lives in Los Angeles. An innately talented chef who can cook a gourmet meal from whatever happens to be in my refrigerator, he's been cooking our family Thanksgiving meals since we were fifteen. Now and then he surprises me with a fabulous dessert made with low-fat ingredients (the Los Angeles influence!), such as this cake with apples and yogurt, which give the cake a dense, moist texture. The caramel-cream cheese frosting is optional; it dresses up the cake and makes it more festive, but the cake is delicious on its own.

FOR THE CAKE

3 cups organic all-purpose flour

2 teaspoons ground organic cinnamon

1 teaspoon baking soda

1 teaspoon baking powder

1 teaspoon salt

1 pound organic or farm-fresh Golden Delicious apples (5 to 6 apples), peeled, cored, and cut into 1/2-inch cubes

8 tablespoons (1 stick) organic unsalted butter

4 teaspoons calvados (optional)

1 cup firmly packed organic dark brown sugar

1 cup organic canola oil

1/4 cup organic plain whole milk yogurt

3 teaspoons organic vanilla extract

6 large organic eggs

1/2 cup organic cane sugar

Preheat the oven to 350°F. Butter and flour a Bundt pan and set aside.

Sift the flours, cinnamon, baking soda, baking powder, and salt together in a medium bowl. Set aside.

Place the apples, butter, and calvados in a saucepan and sauté the apples over medium-high heat for about 10 minutes, until the apples are light brown and cooked. Set aside to cool.

In a large bowl, whisk together the brown sugar, oil, yogurt, and vanilla extract. Add the flour mixture and whisk until mixed.

In a separate bowl, beat the egg whites until slightly thick, then beat in the cane sugar, a little at a time, until the egg mixture is glossy and stiff. Stir a cup of the egg mixture into the batter, then fold in the remaining egg mixture. Stir in the apple mixture, and transfer the batter to the prepared Bundt pan.

Bake until a tester comes out clean, about 1 hour.

Let cool in the pan for 20 minutes, then invert onto a wire rack to cool completely. Top with caramel–cream cheese frosting.

caramel–cream cheese frosting

| MAKES 2 CUPS |

The harmony of caramel and apples makes this frosting a perfect match for the cake.

1 stick (^{1}/2 cup) organic unsalted butter
1 cup organic brown sugar

^{1}/4 cup organic whole milk
8 ounces organic cream cheese, cold

Melt the butter in a small heavy skillet over medium heat. Whisk in the sugar, stirring until it dissolves and darkens, 8 to 10 minutes. Slowly pour the milk in, and continue to mix for a few minutes. Remove from the heat and let cool.

Place the cream cheese in a bowl, breaking it into small pieces. Pour in the caramel and beat until the mixture is smooth, about 3 minutes.

Refrigerate the frosting for 30 minutes before spreading it on the cake. If the frosting is too thick, allow it to stand at room temperature to soften. Reserve 1 cup frosting for the piping, if you will be decorating the cake.

to decorate | To MAKE THE CAKE pictured on page 52, quadruple the recipe, in two 8-inch pans, and 2 6-inch pans. Triple the caramel–cream cheese frosting as well. Because this cake contains chunks of apples, don't try slicing it into thinner layers, or you'll have a mess on your hands. Fill and frost the cakes, then chill. Follow the directions for tiering a cake on page 242, and then your cake is ready to decorate.

When I make this cake for the Jewish New Year (Rosh Hashanah), I get fancy and make little "apple blossoms." First make gold luster paint (see page 238) and hand-paint branches onto the cake. Use avocado green luster dust (see page 238) to paint leaves on the branches. Then place light pink or white gumpaste flowers off the painted branches, in a pretty, diagonal direction. I pipe small yellow stamens in the flowers and scatter yellow gumpaste honeybees (see page 230) around them. If I don't have time to make flowers, I do a honey drizzle. Just warm 1/2 cup honey in the microwave and pour it into a plastic sandwich bag. Snip a small opening in the corner of the bag, drizzle the honey over the cake, and chill. You can top this au natural look with a cluster of small crab apples and leaves, which can be found at most farmers' markets in the fall.

pineapple upside down cake
w/ cherries + nuts

Clyde picked me a yellow flower at the
park, came home and baked this cake
then.

pineapple upside-down cake

| MAKES ONE 9—INCH CAKE |

This cake was a hit at my early Brooklyn dinner parties, especially since I used to be pretty heavy-handed with the rum. Now that I serve the cake at dinners where there are kids, I tend not to include the booze. I add pureed pineapple to the batter, so it's super-moist and tangy. Fresh pineapple gives this cake amazing flavor, and you can use the excess fruit for other delicious recipes such as the Carrot Cake with Cream Cheese—Lemon Zest Frosting (page 90).

FOR THE GOOEY TOPPING

1 stick ($^1/_2$ cup) organic unsalted butter

2 tablespoons rum (very optional but delicious when serving at adult parties)

1 cup firmly packed organic dark—brown sugar

1 organic pineapple, peeled, cored, and cut into $^1/_2$—inch rings (in a pinch, a 6—ounce can of organic pineapple rings will do)

$^1/_4$ teaspoon salt

Handful of dried sour cherries (less than $^1/_4$ cup), soaked in hot water for 20 minutes to plump, then drained

$^1/_4$ cup chopped toasted organic pecans

FOR THE CAKE

1 $^1/_2$ cups organic all—purpose flour

2 teaspoons organic ground cinnamon

2 teaspoons baking powder

$^1/_4$ teaspoon salt

1 stick ($^1/_2$ cup) organic unsalted butter, softened

1 cup organic cane sugar

2 large organic eggs

1 teaspoon organic vanilla extract

4 tablespoons rum (again, optional)

$^1/_2$ cup finely chopped organic pineapple (see Note)

Prepare the topping: In a 9-inch iron skillet (or my personal favorite, a 9-inch All-Clad sauté pan), stir the butter, rum (if using), salt, and brown sugar over medium heat until melted, about 4 minutes. Remove from the heat and arrange the pineapple slices in the skillet in a circle, or cut the rings up for another design option. Place 2 or 3 cherries in the center of each pineapple ring and scatter the rest around the pineapple slices (think about those funny old pictures of maraschino cherries on an upside-down cake). Reserve the leftover pineapple for the cake batter. Scatter the nuts evenly over the pineapple and cherries. Set aside while you make the cake batter.

Preheat the oven to 350°F.

In a medium bowl, sift together the flour, cinnamon, baking powder, and salt. Set aside.

In a standing mixer fitted with the whisk attachment, cream the butter and sugar on medium speed until fluffy, about 3 minutes. Add the eggs, one at a time, and beat until incorporated, making sure to scrape down the sides of the bowl with a spatula as you go along. Add the vanilla and 2 tablespoons of the rum (if using).

With the mixer on low speed, alternate adding the flour mixture and the pureed pineapple, starting and ending with the flour. Use a rubber spatula to scrape the batter over the gooey topping in the skillet.

Bake for 40 to 45 minutes, or until a tester inserted in the center comes out clean. The cake should be a light golden brown. Be careful, as the hot gooey topping may be bubbling up. Let cool in the skillet for about 10 minutes.

Place a serving plate upside down over the skillet, and flip them over together to invert the cake, taking care to avoid touching the hot topping. Pour any excess juices on top. Sprinkle the remaining 2 table-spoons rum, if using, over the cake. Let cool to room temperature.

Note: Use the remaining pineapple from the gooey topping. My preference is to puree it in a food processor.

to decorate | SINCE THIS CAKE is a work of art on its own, simply place it on a pretty glass plate or platter and then on a cake stand for some height. Add rum to Vanilla Whipped Cream (page 180) and serve a dollop on top.

red velvet love cake

This is the recipe for my wedding cake, a bright red cake that says "love" in the prettiest way. I believe that whatever love you put into the cake can be tasted. Our friends baked it for us, and instead of an elaborate decoration or cake topper, they used organic wildflowers to cover the cake, which went along with the casual tone of our wedding. It was just perfect. Every year I bake this cake for our anniversary, to remind us of our sweetest day.

I tried using beet dye and other natural food colorings, but nothing beats a professional-grade red food coloring to make the cake really red. The cake looks sweet when you bake it in a heart shape, either as a large cake or as cupcakes. For the cupcakes, I like to squeeze a little of the frosting inside for a surprising, yummy center (see page 143).

3 cups organic all—purpose flour

1/2 teaspoon salt

1 1/2 tablespoons organic unsweetened
    cocoa powder

2 teaspoons vinegar

2 teaspoons baking soda

2 sticks (1 cup) organic unsalted butter,
    softened

2 cups organic cane sugar

3 large organic eggs

1 1/2 cups organic buttermilk

1 1/2 tablespoons organic vanilla extract

2 tablespoons (1 ounce) professional red
    food coloring, such as "Super Red" or
    "Tulip Red" (see Note)

Vanilla Whipped Buttercream (page 84)

Preheat the oven to 350°F. Butter and flour two 8-inch round cake pans, or place liners in 2 muffin pans for 24 cupcakes. Set aside.

Sift the flour and salt together into a large bowl. Set aside.

In a small bowl, mix the cocoa powder, vinegar, and baking soda together. Set aside.

In a standing mixer fitted with the paddle attachment, beat the butter and sugar on medium speed until light and fluffy, 3 to 4 minutes. Add the eggs, one at a time, and continue mixing until well blended. Mix in the buttermilk, vanilla, and food coloring. Then add the cocoa powder mixture.

With the mixer on low speed, gradually add the dry ingredients to the buttermilk mixture.

Pour the batter into the prepared pans.

Bake for 25 minutes, or until a tester inserted in the center comes out clean. Bake cupcakes for 14 to 16 minutes, checking with a cake tester or a toothpick.

Let the cake cool in the pan for 10 minutes. Then turn it out onto a wire rack and let cool completely.

Frost with the Vanilla Whipped Buttercream.

to decorate | TINT SOME OF THE FROSTING pink and pipe polka dots or hearts all over, or simply decorate the cake with organic flowers (these can be found at a farmers' market).

Note: Sometimes I add a squirt of fuchsia to the mix to make the red a little more pinkish. It's important to use professional food coloring to achieve a bright red color.

flourless chocolate almond cake

When my good friend Gina turned thirty, I had to whip up a fabulous creation. She is gluten-intolerant and a hard-core yoga teacher, so she rarely indulges in sweets the way I do. I wanted to make something really special and divine, and I knew that the road to a decent flourless cake is paved in ground nuts. This cake is moist, gooey, and rich. It goes well with fresh berries and Vanilla Whipped Cream (page 180).

FOR THE CAKE

8 ounces organic 70% dark chocolate

2 sticks (1 cup) organic unsalted butter

1 teaspoon instant organic coffee dissolved
    in 1 teaspoon hot water or a 1-teaspoon
    shot of espresso

1 1/2 cups ground toasted organic almonds
    (from about 1 1/2 cups almonds; see box,
    page 65)

3/4 cup firmly packed organic dark-brown
    sugar

2 teaspoons organic vanilla extract

6 organic eggs, separated

1/2 teaspoon salt

2 tablespoons organic cane sugar

FOR THE SHINY MOCHA GLAZE

1-ounce bags semisweet organic chocolate chips

6 tablespoons (3/4 stick) organic unsalted
    butter, softened, cut into pieces

2 teaspoons organic instant coffee,
    dissolved in 1/2 cup hot organic heavy
    cream

Preheat the oven to 350°F. Butter the bottom and sides of a 10-inch round cake pan, and line the bottom of the pan with parchment paper. Set aside.

Melt the chocolate, butter, and dissolved coffee in the top of a small double boiler set over medium heat. Stir until just melted and smooth. Remove from the heat and set aside to cool.

In a medium bowl, combine the egg yolks, ground almonds, cooled chocolate mixture, brown sugar, and vanilla extract, whisking to combine. Set aside.

In a standing mixer or using a hand mixer, beat the egg whites on low speed until bubbles start to form. Add the salt to the whites and gradually increase the speed to medium-high. As the eggs become white, slowly add the sugar, beating until the whites are glossy and can hold a firm peak. Using a rubber spatula, stir one large spoonful of the whites into the almond-chocolate mixture. Fold in the remaining egg whites in three additions, until white streaks are barely visible.

Pour the batter into the prepared pan, leveling the top of the mixture with a spatula.

Bake for 40 minutes, or until a tester inserted in the center comes out clean.

Once the cake reaches room temperature, cover it with aluminum foil and chill it in the refrigerator for up to 3 hours.

While the cake is chilling, prepare the Shiny Mocha Glaze: Combine the chocolate and butter in a medium stainless-steel bowl, set on a double boiler. Stir until almost melted, then add the hot cream with the coffee dissolved in it. Let cool to warm before frosting the cake.

Using a rubber spatula, spread a spoonful of the warm glaze on top of the chilled cake. Using a small offset spatula, smooth it across the top and sides. Refrigerate the cake for about 15 minutes to set the glaze. Serve immediately, or keep the cake refrigerated, removing it from the refrigerator 1 1/2 hours before serving.

| *frosting*

to decorate | Once the glaze hardens, brush the top and sides of the cake with gold metallic powder (see page 238).

Toasting and Grinding Almonds

Preheat the oven to 350°F. Spread 2 cups whole almonds in one layer in a baking pan, and toast in the middle of the oven for 12 to 14 minutes, or until the skins start to darken and toast. Rub the almonds in a damp dishtowel to remove most of the skin. It's okay if some skin remains. Let cool completely before grinding. In small batches, grind the almonds in a clean coffee grinder, mini food processor, or nut grinder until fine and powdery, taking care to make sure that the nuts near the blade don't get too hot and turn into almond butter! Extra ground almonds can be stored in the freezer for up to 3 months.

blanca cake

With no egg yolks in it, the Blanca Cake is truly "white," so the batter is a perfect blank canvas to tint an array of colors. I use this cake for regal events—weddings, anniversaries, large parties—and typically frost it in bright colors to make a stunning impact.

2 cups organic all-purpose flour

2 teaspoons baking powder

1 teaspoon salt

3 sticks (1 $^1/_2$ cups) organic unsalted
    butter, softened

2 $^1/_4$ cups organic cane sugar

1 tablespoon organic vanilla extract

1 cup organic whole milk

7 organic egg whites

Preheat the oven to 350°F. Butter two 8-inch round cake pans, and line the bottoms with parchment paper rounds. Butter the parchment, dust with flour, tap out the excess flour, and set aside. For cupcakes, you will need 3 muffin pans for 30 cupcakes; either bake in batches or if you have 3 pans, use them at the same time. For the tray that is incomplete, fill the empty cupcake spaces halfway with water to prevent the cupcakes in that tray from overbaking.

In a medium bowl, sift together the flour, baking powder, and salt. Set aside.

In a standing mixer fitted with the paddle attachment, beat the butter and 2 cups of the sugar on medium speed until light and fluffy, 3 to 4 minutes, using a rubber spatula to scrape the sides of the bowl.

In a small bowl, combine the vanilla and milk. Set aside.

With the mixer on low speed, add the flour mixture in three parts, alternating with the milk mixture, beginning and ending with the flour mixture.

In a clean bowl, use a hand mixer or a clean standing mixer to beat the egg whites on low speed until they become foamy. Slowly pour in the remaining $\frac{1}{4}$ cup sugar and gradually increase the speed to medium-high. Beat until the whites are shiny, with stiff glossy peaks. Be careful not to overbeat.

Using a rubber spatula, gently fold a third of the whites into the cake batter. Then, in two additions, fold in the remaining whites just until the streaks of white are incorporated.

Divide the batter evenly between the prepared pans, smoothing the tops with an offset spatula. Bake until the cakes are golden brown and a tester inserted in the center comes out clean, around 35 minutes. For cupcakes, test them after around 24 minutes.

Let the cakes cool in the pans, set on a wire cooling rack, for 20 minutes. Then invert the cakes onto the rack, peel off the parchment, and turn them over so the tops are facing up. Let cool completely.

filling and frosting |

Fill and frost this cake with your favorite combinations, such as Red Currant Curd (page 92) for filling and Dark-Chocolate Secret Frosting (page 87) for frosting, or Espresso Whipped Buttercream (page 85) for filling and Marshmallow Frosting (page 88), tinted bright fuchsia, as frosting.

to decorate | To make the cake pictured on page 67, prepare sugar paste butterflies and flowers (page 229) a few days before serving the cake, tinting the sugar paste light gray for the butterflies and fuchsia for subtly whimsical flowers. Hand-paint the butterflies (see page 231) if desired, using edible food markers, paint made from food coloring, or metallic luster mixed with alcohol. For small flowers, I use a mix of cutters within the same size range.

Fill the cake with a desired filling, and for the frosting, tint one batch of vanilla whipped cream fuchsia. Do a thin crumb coat, chill, and then repeat the frosting with a thicker layer to cover the entire cake. Let chill for 15 minutes. Place the flowers on the cake in a diagonal direction from a corner on top to the opposite corner on the bottom of the cake. Scatter the butterflies around the flowers as though they're fluttering away. Tint the remaining fuchsia frosting black by adding super black food coloring. Fit the piping bag with the 1 tip, and pipe stamen inside the flowers.

If you're making cupcakes, frost the cupcakes with fuchsia buttercream in big swirls (page 234). Place the cupcakes on a cake stand, decorate them with clusters of three small flowers, and pipe with dark centers. Place single small butterflies on some of the cupcakes.

lovely lemon cake

| MAKES ONE 8− OR 9−INCH BOWL−SHAPED CAKE, ONE 8−INCH LAYER CAKE,

OR 26 TO 28 CUPCAKES |

Every winter I visit California to escape New York's chill. After defrosting in the sun, I like to raid my parents' Meyer lemon tree and bake endless batches of lemon cake and lemon-lime bars. Coming home, I just have to remember to leave some room in my suitcase for my clothes!

To make this cake a little more interesting and grand, I like to bake it in an 8- or 9-inch stainless-steel bowl. The size of your bowl can vary slightly, but keep a close watch on the cake—it might need a little more baking time. The cake looks beautiful with large swirls of lemony Marshmallow Frosting piped on top, with bits of candied lemon or lemon slices for garnish. The lemon syrup adds an infusion of lemon flavor too.

2 sticks (1 cup) organic unsalted butter,
    softened

2 cups organic cane sugar

Gated zest of 4 organic Meyer lemons
    (1 heaping tablespoon)

3 large organic eggs

1 tablespoon organic vanilla extract

3 cups organic all−purpose flour

$1/2$ teaspoon baking soda

$1/2$ teaspoon baking powder

$1/2$ teaspoon salt

1 cup organic buttermilk

$1/2$ cup fresh organic Meyer lemon juice
    (from the zested lemons)

Lemon Syrup

Simple Lemon Glaze (page 74) or
    Marshmallow Frosting (page 88)

Preheat the oven to 350°F. Butter and flour an 8- or 9-inch stainless-steel bowl or two 8- or 9-inch round cake pans. For cupcakes, line 3 muffin tins with liners, making sure to fill empty cupcake areas halfway with water to prevent burning. Set aside.

In a standing mixer fitted with the whisk attachment, cream the butter, sugar, and lemon zest on medium-high speed for 3 minutes. Use a rubber spatula to scrape down the sides of the bowl.

Add the eggs, one at a time, stirring until mixed. Then add the vanilla extract.

In a medium bowl, sift the flour, baking soda, baking powder, and salt together. Set aside.

Mix the buttermilk and lemon juice together in a small bowl. Set aside.

With the mixer on a low speed, alternate adding the dry and wet ingredients in three separate additions, beating until combined.

Pour the batter into the prepared bowl or pans. If using a bowl, place it on a baking sheet to make it easy to insert and remove from the oven. Bake for 50 to 55 minutes, or until a tester inserted in the center comes out clean. If you're baking this in traditional cake pans, the baking time is a little shorter: 35 to 40 minutes. Cupcake time is 25 to 30 minutes.

If you will be using the lemon syrup, prepare it while the cake is baking so that it's ready when the cake is done.

Remove the pan(s) from the oven. If you baked the cake in a bowl, set the bowl on a wire rack and let the cake cool for 20 minutes, then invert it onto a plate and remove it from the bowl. If you used two standard cake pans, let the cakes cool in the pans for 20 minutes, then remove the cakes and let them cool on a wire rack. For cupcakes, remove from the tins and let cool completely on a wire rack.

If you are using the lemon syrup, poke some holes in the warm cake with a cake tester or a toothpick and pour the warm syrup over the cake. Let the cake cool completely.

filling and frosting |

If you baked two standard layers, blend Marshmallow Frosting with
1 tablespoon grated lemon zest, and spread the frosting between the
layers and over the top and sides. Or spread the frosting between
the layers and top the cake with the Simple Lemon Glaze. If you
baked a bowl-shaped cake, top it with the lemony Marshmallow
Frosting or with the Lemon Glaze. For cupcakes, remove from the
pans and let cool completely on a wire rack.

to decorate | ARRANGE CANDIED LEMON SLICES (page 74), overlapping, in a
circle on top of the Lemon Glaze–topped cake.

Fit a pastry bag with a large rounded tip and pipe small circles in
rows around the cake. Place Candied Lemon Slices on top of some
of the rounds to give the cake a polka-dot look.

lemon syrup

1 cup organic cane sugar
1/2 cup fresh organic Meyer lemon juice

Combine the sugar and lemon juice in a small saucepan and bring
to a boil. Boil for 1 minute, and then remove from the heat.

simple lemon glaze

This lemon glaze is a classic lemon–cake topping. Use the glaze after the cake has cooled, or else it will melt into the cake!

2 cups organic powdered sugar
3 tablespoons fresh organic lemon juice
1/2 teaspoon organic vanilla extract

Whisk all the ingredients together in a bowl.

Once the cake has cooled, pour the mixture on top, using the back of a spoon to coax it to drip down the sides in the direction you desire. If you want to give the cake a splattered Jackson Pollock look, tint the glaze with a variety of colors and use the tines of a fork to design splotches.

candied lemon slices

This is a fun, rustic way to decorate with lemons. If you plan on eating the peel, however, make sure you use organic fruit, which isn't waxed or sprayed with pesticides.

3 medium organic lemons
1 cup organic cane sugar

Slice the lemons as thin as possible, about 1/8 inch thick, and remove any seeds.

Cut sheets of wax paper and place them underneath a wire cooling rack.

Combine the sugar and 1 cup water in a small heavy-bottomed saucepan, and cook over high heat until the sugar dissolves and the mixture is boiling. Add the lemon slices and let the mixture simmer over medium-low heat for 15 minutes, or until the lemon slices are opaque. Make sure the sugar mixture does not begin to caramelize.

Using a fork or a slotted spoon, carefully transfer the lemon slices to the wire cooling rack, arranging them in a single layer. Let them dry for at least 1 hour. The lemon slices should be slightly sticky.

Extra slices, placed between pieces of wax or parchment paper and placed in an airtight container, can be frozen for up to 2 weeks or refrigerated for 1 week.

Note: Use limes instead of lemons to make Candied Lime Slices for Lemon–Lime Bars (page 127).

lotus cake

The cake layers are subtly flavored with an orange-flower water syrup to raise the sophis-
tication level, and the decoration is a lotus flower, which grows in bright, colorful, sunny
India.

FOR THE CAKE
3 1/2 cups plus 2 tablespoons organic all—
   purpose flour
1 teaspoon salt
1/4 cup baking powder
1/2 cup organic whole milk
1 cup buttermilk

2 1/2 sticks unsalted organic butter,
   softened
2 cups organic cane sugar
3 tablespoons grated organic orange zest
1 tablespoon organic vanilla extract
8 egg whites
Vanilla Whipped Buttercream (page 84)

ORANGE—FLOWER WATER SYRUP
1/2 cup organic cane sugar
1/4 cup organic orange juice

1/4 cup orange—flower water
1 teaspoon grated organic orange zest

Preheat the oven to 350°F. Butter and flour two cake pans—an
8-inch and a 6-inch pan, both at least 3 inches high. Cut out parchment paper and place on the bottoms of the pans to prevent the
cakes from sticking. Set aside.

Sift the flour, salt, and baking powder together in a bowl and set
aside.

Combine the milk, buttermilk, and vanilla in a separate bowl and
set aside.

In a standing mixer or using a handheld mixer, cream the butter and 1 ½ cups of the sugar until light and fluffy, about 3 minutes.

Combine the orange zest with the butter/sugar mixture.

In 5 additions, starting and ending with the flour mixture, mix the flour and milk mixtures into the butter/sugar mixture.

When the ingredients are just combined, pour the batter into a separate large bowl and set aside.

Carefully clean the beaters and the bowl to prepare for beating the egg whites.

Beat the whites on low speed until bubbles form, then increase the speed to medium-high. Once the egg whites are almost peaking, slowly add the remaining ½ cup sugar, beating the egg whites until they're glossy but not too stiff.

Gently mix ½ cup of the egg whites into the batter to lighten it up. Carefully fold in the remaining egg whites until just combined. It's okay if the batter looks slightly curdled.

Pour the batter into the prepared cake pans. Bake for 45 to 50 minutes, or until a cake tester or a toothpick comes out clean.

Let the cakes cool in the pan for 15 minutes, then turn over onto a wire rack, remove the parchment paper, and let cool completely.

TO PREPARE THE SYRUP

In a small heavy-bottomed saucepan over medium-high heat, bring the syrup ingredients to a simmer for 5 minutes. Let cool to room temperature.

TO ASSEMBLE

Cut each cake into 3 layers. Prepare 1 1/2 batches of Vanilla Whipped Buttercream. Place each layer on a cake round and brush them with the orange-flower water syrup. Spread 1/4 cup Vanilla Whipped Buttercream onto 2 of the 3 layers of each cake. Stack the layers so that you have 2 cakes, each with 3 cake layers and 2 buttercream layers.

Place in the refrigerator to chill for about 20 minutes.

To make a crumb coat, cover each cake with a thin layer of Vanilla Whipped Buttercream. Chill again in the refrigerator for 15 minutes.

While the cake is chilling, fill two small bowls with about 3/4 cup frosting each. Dip a toothpick in the deep pink food color, and add one drop to one of the small bowls. Mix with a spoon until the frosting is hot pink. Tint the orange frosting the same way.

Fill two small pastry bags, with couplers, with the two frostings, and fit each with a number-12 tip. (If you have only one tip, you can do one color at a time, washing out the tip for the second color.) Remove the chilled cake layers from the refrigerator and pipe a thick line of orange frosting around the bottom of each one, about 1/4 inch from the cake. Pipe a thick line of the hot-pink frosting right above the line of orange frosting.

Frost the tops and sides of both cake layers with the remaining white buttercream, almost touching the hot-pink-frosted line. Then, holding a large clean spatula vertically next to one of the layers, with the bottom tip of the spatula almost touching the bottom of the cake and applying slight pressure, move the spatula in a continuous motion around the cake, so that the orange, pink, and white frostings blend into one another. Try not to lift the spatula until you reach the starting point. If you need to to go back and blend the frostings, use a smaller spatula and blend where needed. For a chic finish, sprinkle and press the edible orange glitter toward the bottom of the cake halves.

Chill the cake for 15 minutes. Then remove it from the refrigerator and follow the instructions for tiering the cake (page 242). Place the smaller cake on top, centering it evenly. Place the lotus flower on the top tier. Refrigerate until ready to serve.

lotus flower

The lotus flower should be made at least a week to 2 days before the cake so that it has time to dry.

3/4 cup homemade gumpaste (see page 223)

1 container (4 grams) orange petal dust

1 container (4 grams) lilac petal dust

1 container (4 grams) brown luster dust

About 1 tablespoon Vanilla Whipped
  Buttercream (page 84)

Roll out the gumpaste. Pinch off a small amount, shape it into a cone, and set it aside to dry.

Using rose-leaf cutters or a small sharp knife, cut out pointed-edge petals, making three sizes: small, medium, and large. Using a silicone veiner (see page 232), make a slight impression on each petal.

Dry the petals in an empty egg carton (lined with plastic wrap) so that each petal can curve slightly; or set a drinking glass on its side, cover it with plastic wrap, and dry the petals on the curved glass.

Once the petals have dried, brush orange petal dust and lilac petal dust onto the petals, dusting half in orange and the other half in lilac. Use brown luster on the edges and backs for a rustic effect.

Arrange the larger petals, overlapping slightly, in a circle to form the base of the flower. Set the small cone in the center of the large petals, and gradually build the flower, using the vanilla buttercream as glue to hold the petal bases in place. Keep adding the medium, and then the small, petals until the flower is full and pretty.

Let the flower dry in a cool place.

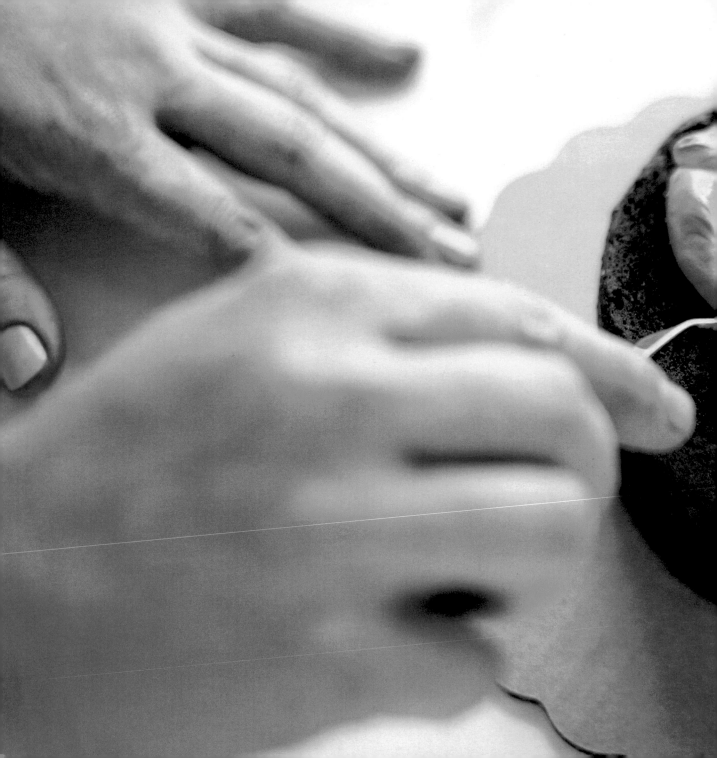

frostings,
fillings,
and curds

frostings and fillings

Although I like to experiment with wild flavors and combinations in my baking, when it comes to a cake that everyone can really obsess over, I find that simplicity rules. These are my basic, tried-and-true frostings and fillings that complement a variety of cakes. All you have to do is mix and match them for a cake that tastes unique.

vanilla whipped buttercream

| MAKES 3 ¹⁄₂ CUPS FROSTING, ENOUGH TO FROST AND FILL ONE 8—INCH LAYER CAKE OR TO FROST 24 CUPCAKES |

I love using this as a frosting or a filling because it is light and creamy, and less sweet than the Classic Americana Icing. It tastes just like whipped cream.

2 sticks (1 cup) organic unsalted butter, softened

1 cup organic cane sugar

1 cup organic whole milk

¹⁄₄ cup sifted organic all—purpose flour

1 ¹⁄₂ tablespoons organic vanilla extract

Cream the butter on medium speed, 3 to 5 minutes, in a standing mixer or with a hand mixer until soft, about 30 seconds. Add the sugar and beat on high speed until light and fluffy, 5 to 7 minutes.

In a small saucepan, combine ¹⁄₄ cup of the milk, the flour, and the vanilla extract, and whisk until there are no lumps. Over medium heat, slowly add the remaining ³⁄₄ cup milk, whisking constantly, and cook until the mixture comes to a low boil. Then reduce the heat to low and keep whisking for a few more minutes, until the mixture starts to thicken.

Immediately remove the pan from the heat, but keep stirring. (After you have removed the pan from the heat, the mixture will continue to cook for a minute or two on its own. If you overheat it and get small lumps, try to whisk vigorously to get them out, or pass the mixture through a fine-mesh sieve.) If necessary, place the pan over a bowl of ice water to stop the cooking process and allow the mixture to cool.

Once the milk mixture has thickened, set it aside to cool to room temperature. You can stick it in the freezer to rush the cooling.

With the mixer on low speed, slowly pour the milk mixture into the butter-sugar mixture. Increase the speed to medium and beat until the frosting is light and fluffy, 3 to 5 minutes. Add vanilla to combine.

Espresso Whipped Buttercream

This version works beautifully as a filling with a dark-chocolate frosting—you get the best of both worlds: Dissolve 1 heaping teaspoon instant espresso powder in 1 tablespoon boiling water. Combine with the butter-sugar mixture.

Chocolate Whipped Buttercream

This light and fluffy chocolate frosting tastes like whipped cream with a hint of chocolate: While the milk mixture is cooling, melt 4 ounces unsweetened or dark chocolate in the top of a double boiler set over simmering water, or in 30-second bursts in a microwave. Cool to room temperature. With the mixer on low speed, combine the chocolate with the butter-sugar mixture.

classic americana icing

| MAKES 4 CUPS FROSTING, ENOUGH TO FILL AND FROST ONE 8—INCH LAYER CAKE OR TO FROST 24 CUPCAKES |

This buttery, super-sweet, sugary icing is quick and easy to make. You always can substitute the vanilla extract for other flavors, such as almond, peppermint, or orange, to give your cake an unexpected twist.

2 sticks (1 cup) organic unsalted butter

7 cups (about 1 $^3/_4$ pounds) organic powdered sugar, sifted

3 tablespoons organic whole milk

1 $^1/_2$ tablespoons organic vanilla extract

In an electric mixer with a whisk attachment, whip the butter on medium speed until pale and fluffy, about 3 minutes.

Add 4 cups of the sifted powdered sugar and mix on low speed, scraping down the sides of the bowl while combining. Raise the speed to medium for 30 seconds.

On low speed, add the milk and mix until combined. Add the remaining powdered sugar and scrape down the sides of the bowl.

Add the vanilla extract and scrape the sides again. If the frosting seems too soft, add more powdered sugar in $^1/_2$-cup increments until it becomes thick and fluffy.

Chocolate Americana Icing

Melt 4 ounces unsweetened organic chocolate in the top of a double boiler set over simmering water, or in 30-second bursts in a microwave. Cool to room temperature. Combine the cooled melted chocolate with the whipped butter before adding the sugar.

dark–chocolate secret frosting

| MAKES 3 CUPS FROSTING, ENOUGH TO FILL AND FROST ONE 8–INCH LAYER
CAKE OR TO FROST 24 CUPCAKES |

Adding sour cream to cakes and frostings keeps them moist and offsets the sweetness a bit. I use the word "secret" here because some people, like my husband, hate sour cream. When I bake with it or use it in this dark–chocolate frosting, he licks his plate clean. I think it's all psychological, so until he goes into therapy and is released from his neurosis, I'll just keep it a secret!

I like this frosting's sophisticated, not overly sugary taste. I most often make it as a filling or frosting for the Blanca Cake (page 66) or the Diablo Cake (page 39).

8 ounces organic unsweetened chocolate

1 stick ($^1/_2$ cup) unsalted organic butter, cut into small pieces

1 $^1/_2$ tablespoons organic vanilla extract

Pinch of sea salt

2 $^1/_2$ cups sifted organic powdered sugar

$^3/_4$ cup organic sour cream

Melt the chocolate and butter together in the top of a double boiler set over simmering water, or in short bursts in a microwave, stirring until thoroughly melted and combined. Set aside to cool.

In a standing mixer fitted with the paddle attachment, combine the chocolate-butter mixture, vanilla extract, and sea salt on low speed. Slowly add the powdered sugar and continue beating on low speed until the ingredients are combined.

Add the sour cream, increase the speed to medium, and beat until thickened, around 6 minutes. Use immediately and then put the cake or cupcakes in the refrigerator for 15 minutes to set the frosting.

marshmallow frosting

This fluffy, thick, creamy frosting tastes just like marshmallows. For a striking effect, tint it bright colors and pipe it in oversized swirls on cupcakes (see page 234).

When you prepare the frosting, be sure to work quickly, because it sets with a soft shine that will disappear if retouched. You'll need a standing mixer and a candy thermometer, because the sugar has to be heated to 236°F to create a marshmallow-like consistency.

6 organic egg whites
1 $\frac{1}{2}$ cups organic cane sugar
$\frac{1}{4}$ teaspoon cream of tartar

1 $\frac{1}{2}$ tablespoons organic vanilla extract
Food coloring (optional)

Clean a standing mixer according to the directions in "Golden Rules and Tips for Cakes and Cupcakes" (page 27). Place the egg whites in the mixing bowl.

In a small heavy-bottomed saucepan, stir together the sugar, cream of tartar, and $\frac{2}{3}$ cup water, and bring to a boil over high heat.

When a candy thermometer inserted into the sugar mixture reads 230°F, whip the egg whites on low speed for about 30 seconds, until bubbly. Increase the mixer speed to medium-high and whip the whites for 2 minutes.

With the mixer still running, check the temperature of your sugar mixture. When the thermometer reads around 235°F, increase the mixer speed to high and whip the egg whites until they're almost stiff. At the same time, remove the boiling sugar mixture from the heat.

Standing as far as you can from the mixer, with arms extended to avoid burning yourself, pour the hot sugar in a small stream into the running mixer. Keep the mixer on high speed for at least 5 minutes.

Reduce the mixer speed to low and add the vanilla extract and optional food coloring. (To tint the frosting different colors, quickly divide the frosting among separate bowls and add food coloring as desired.)

If using, fill the piping bag immediately, or frost the cake immediately.

cream cheese–lemon zest frosting

| MAKES 4 1/2 CUPS FROSTING, ENOUGH TO FILL AND FROST ONE 8–INCH LAYER CAKE OR TO FROST 24 CUPCAKES |

This is a great frosting for the Carrot Cake (page 45) or the Lovely Lemon Cake (page 70). The lemon zest complements the cream cheese so perfectly that I sometimes even snack on this frosting—I just can't get enough of the sweet, tangy flavor! If you want extra oomph on the Carrot Cake, add minced ginger to the lemon zest.

Three 8–ounce packages organic cream cheese, softened
2 sticks (1 cup) organic unsalted butter, softened

1 teaspoon grated organic lemon zest
1 1/2 tablespoons fresh organic lemon juice
1 tablespoon organic vanilla extract
2 3/4 cups organic powdered sugar

In a standing mixer fitted with the whisk attachment, whip the cream cheese and butter on medium-high speed until combined and airy, about 2 minutes. Mix in the lemon zest, lemon juice, and vanilla.

Sift the powdered sugar onto a piece of parchment or wax paper. With the mixer on low speed, slowly pour the sifted powdered sugar into the frosting (use both hands to bend the paper so the sugar pours slowly into the bowl).

Scrape down the sides of the bowl with a rubber spatula. If the frosting seems too soft to spread, allow it to chill for 15 minutes in the refrigerator.

mocha buttercream

| MAKES 3 CUPS FROSTING, ENOUGH TO FILL AND FROST ONE 8—INCH LAYER CAKE OR TO FROST 24 CUPCAKES |

My personal favorite, this frosting is thick and creamy but not cloying. The secret is the egg yolks, which have been used since the 1950s to thicken frostings and create a velvety texture without requiring lots of butter. When choosing this frosting, be aware that many pregnant women are cautious about eating uncooked eggs.

6 ounces organic unsweetened chocolate
2 sticks (1 cup) organic unsalted butter, softened
1 teaspoon organic vanilla extract

1 tablespoon organic instant coffee, dissolved in 2 tablespoons hot water
2 organic egg yolks
Pinch of salt

Melt the chocolate either in the microwave (see baking tools, page 247) or in the top of a double boiler set over simmering water, stirring it frequently with a rubber spatula. Remove the chocolate from the heat and set aside to cool.

Using a standing or hand mixer on medium speed, cream the butter until fluffy, around 3 minutes.

Mix the vanilla extract, coffee, salt, and melted chocolate into the butter. Add the egg yolks, one at a time, and beat on medium speed for 1 minute.

Fill and or frost your cake, and chill it in the refrigerator for 15 minutes for the frosting to set.

chic curds

These curds are chic because they have strong, bold flavors that add dimension to each bite of cake. Made from local farm-fresh ingredients, such as red currants, Meyer lemons, and grapefruit, these curds have the consistency of a custard, and can be used between cake layers, on their own (as I prefer), or alternating with frosting. They can also be served as a dessert in a fancy goblet with fresh whipped cream and a slice of cake on the side.

red currant curd

| MAKES 1 1/2 CUPS, ENOUGH TO FILL ONE 8-INCH LAYER CAKE AND HAVE A FEW EXTRA SPOONFULS AS A TREAT |

Red currants, black currants, and gooseberries have a brief but glorious season in the summer—usually only a few weeks in July. When they appear, I love to make this fancy curd. Currants have a distinctive flavor not commonly found in a curd, and they impart a beautiful crimson color. This tangy curd makes an amazing filling for Chocolate Love Blossom (page 31) or Blanca Cake (page 66). Or, with a few of Clyde's Sugar Cookies (page 193) on the side, layer it with whipped cream in a wineglass for a fancy dessert.

2 cups organic farm-fresh red currants, gooseberries, or black currants (about 1 pint), rinsed
6 organic egg yolks
1/2 cup organic cane sugar

1 stick (1/2 cup) organic unsalted butter, softened
Pinch of salt
1/2 teaspoon fresh organic lemon juice

In a small heavy-bottomed saucepan, cook the currants or gooseberries in 1/4 cup water over low heat until soft, around 15 minutes. It's okay if there are some stems attached, as they will be strained out.

Strain the currants or gooseberries through a strainer into a medium glass bowl, pressing to get all the juice out, and discard the pulp. Let cool. Rinse the strainer because you'll be using it again.

In the top of a double boiler set over low heat, stir the egg yolks and sugar together. Add the butter and salt, and mix thoroughly. Increase the heat to medium and add the currant or gooseberry puree and the lemon juice.

When the mixture is simmering but not boiling, stir on low to medium heat until thickened, around 5 minutes.

Set the strainer over a glass bowl. Press the curd through the strainer and let it cool to lukewarm.

Cover the curd with plastic wrap, laying the wrap directly on the surface of the curd so that a skin does not form. Refrigerate.

If you're not using the cooled curd immediately, replace the pierced plastic wrap with a fresh unpierced piece, but again press it on top of the curd so a skin doesn't form.

Save Your Egg Yolks for Making Curds!

I like to reuse small yogurt containers for freezing my egg yolks. Pour the yolks into a clean container, cover, and either wrap well with plastic wrap or fit into a freezer bag (this thoroughly insulates the yolks so they won't get freezer burn). You can freeze egg yolks for up to 1 month. When you're ready to use them, allow them to come to room temperature by defrosting them in the refrigerator overnight.

grapefruit curd

Although lemon and lime curds are fine and dandy, I prefer grapefruit, my favorite citrus fruit. Grapefruit Curd works remarkably well as a filling for the Vanilla–Bean Butter Cake (page 37) with Classic Americana Icing (page 86), transforming it into something delightful. If they're in season, look for red grapefruits, which are naturally sweeter. I keep the curd on the tangy side as a filling for cakes.

6 organic egg yolks
1 cup fresh organic grapefruit juice (from 2 or 3 grapefruits, depending on size and juiciness)
Gated zest of 2 organic grapefruits (around 4 tablespoons)

3 tablespoons fresh organic lemon juice
1/2 cup organic cane sugar
1 cup (2 sticks) organic unsalted butter, chilled and cut into small cubes

In a medium bowl, mix the egg yolks, grapefruit juice, half of the grapefruit zest, and the lemon juice until frothy. Stir in the sugar.

Set the bowl in a pot of simmering (not boiling) water, and stir constantly until the mixture thickens, 8 to 10 minutes. Carefully scrape the bottom of the bowl while stirring, or else the egg yolks will cook on the bottom and get lumpy.

Pour the mixture through a fine-mesh sieve into another medium bowl (this gets rid of any bits of egg and ensures a smooth curd). Using a rubber spatula, stir in the butter, one piece at a time, blending well after each addition. Stir in the remaining grapefruit zest.

Cover the bowl with plastic wrap, laying the wrap directly on top of the curd to prevent a skin from forming. Poke a few holes with a knife to let the steam escape. Cool the curd in the refrigerator for a few hours.

If you're not using the cooled curd immediately, replace the pierced plastic wrap with a fresh unpierced piece, but again press it on top of the curd so a skin doesn't form.

Freeze Leftover Egg Whites

If you make curds and have leftover egg whites, you can freeze them for cakes (such as Blanca Cake, page 66) or frosting (such as Marshmallow Frosting, page 88) for up to 1 month in a clean plastic freezer bag placed inside an airtight container. Be sure to mark how many whites you're storing. When you're ready to use the whites, let them defrost in the refrigerator overnight and then bring them to room temperature.

---

meyer lemon curd

| MAKES 2 CUPS OF CURD, ENOUGH TO FILL ONE 8-INCH LAYER CAKE |

Oh, how I love the subtle flavor of Meyer lemons! They grow all over Southern California, as they did wild in the backyard of my childhood home. Growing up, we would make amazing lemonade, lemon bars, and a version of this curd to serve with pound cake. Something like a hybrid of lemons and oranges, Meyer lemons are sweeter than regular lemons, so you don't need to use as much sugar when cooking with them. The Meyer Lemon Curd goes well with the Vanilla-Bean Butter Cake (page 37) or the Lovely Lemon Cake (page 70), or enjoy it on its own in a champagne glass, with farm-fresh blueberries and some whipped cream on top.

1/2 cup organic cane sugar

Grated zest of 3 organic Meyer lemons

3 large organic eggs

5 large organic egg yolks

1 cup fresh organic Meyer lemon juice (from 6 to 7 lemons)

5 ounces (10 tablespoons) organic unsalted butter, chilled and cut into small pieces

Grind the sugar and lemon zest with a mortar and pestle to combine them and release the oils. Transfer the sugar mixture to a medium heatproof bowl, add the eggs and egg yolks, and whisk to combine.

Place the bowl over a saucepan of simmering water and whisk until the sugar has dissolved, about 3 minutes.

Add the lemon juice and continue whisking until the mixture thickens, scraping down the sides of the bowl to make sure the curd is cooking evenly.

Pour the mixture through a fine-mesh sieve into another medium bowl (this gets rid of any bits of egg and ensures a smooth curd).

Using a rubber spatula, stir in the butter, one piece at a time, blending well after each addition.

Cover the bowl with plastic wrap, laying the wrap directly on top of the curd to prevent a skin from forming. Poke a few holes with a knife to let the steam escape. Cool the curd in the refrigerator for a few hours.

If you're not using the cooled curd immediately, replace the pierced plastic wrap with an unpierced fresh piece, but again press it on top of the curd so a skin doesn't form.

cookies and bars

COOKIES ARE THE PERFECT SWEET to eat on the days when you aren't gorging yourself with cake! I love making a batch of dough and freezing half, so I always have the option of fresh-baked cookies when I need my fix. I've included some recipes straight from my family archives, as well as some of the special cookies that I bake each year for holiday parties (not to mention family movie nights on the couch). Cookies have such a wonderful purpose in the universe—they're the perfect gift for new neighbors, they're easy to carry to picnics or parties, they're helpful in the office when you're trying to win everyone over, and most important, they fit perfectly in the secret compartment in Clyde's lunch box. As with cakes, these cookies really stand out when you use organic ingredients, as some have a few sticks of butter in the recipe.

For parties, I like to surround a cake with a tray of cookies, making it easy for guests to nibble without a fork and a plate, Sometimes the beauty of a golden cookie is pretty enough, but there's nothing wrong with sprinkling cookies or bars with a little metallic dust for a dazzling effect.

golden rules and tips for cookies

STOCK UP on cookie cutters year-round, taking advantage of unique shapes that you may find at thrift stores, online, or on sale after the holidays. Copper cutters are stronger than aluminum ones, so they'll retain their shapes better and last longer.

INVEST IN a 1-tablespoon ice cream scooper for your cookie batter—they're available at most kitchenware stores. It makes the measuring process simple, and your hands will never get sticky! This tool also makes your cookies more uniform, so they stack nicely in a box or bag.

A GOOD ROLLING PIN will make cookie rolling a breeze. I like the simple wooden ones, but if you make cookies often, you may want to invest in a rolling pin with a marble body to keep the cookie dough cool as you roll it out.

SILPAT MATS are silicone mats that go on top of any baking sheet and prevent cookies from sticking. Silpats also reduce the need for parchment paper or aluminum foil to make baking more eco-friendly.

MAKE SURE ALL YOUR INGREDIENTS are at the right temperatures when you start. For instance, most cookie recipes call for softened butter.

ALWAYS PREHEAT THE OVEN FULLY before putting your cookies inside.

TO MAKE PERFECT ROLLED COOKIES, such as sugar cookies, cut two sheets of parchment paper the size of a baking sheet. Place half the cookie dough on one sheet of parchment paper and cover it with the second sheet. Use a rolling pin to carefully flatten and even out the dough, close to your desired thickness, taking care not to let the dough squeeze out the sides of the paper. Place briefly in the freezer or refrigerator to quickly chill and harden. When you go to finish rolling the cookies out, you won't need an excessive amount of flour, and the dough will not stick to the roller. This method is my key to baking large amounts of sugar cookies around the holidays.

chocolate explosion cookies

| MAKES 30 COOKIES |

I love making this over-the-top, super-chocolate explosion when I need to indulge my chocolate sweet tooth. I add white chocolate chips and chunks of dark chocolate to a salty chocolate base so each bite is fulfilling. These are so rich and satisfying that it's hard to eat more than three (I've tried!). When you go to the dentist with lots of cavities, perhaps bring a batch of these so that he or she can understand. They also make excellent cookies for ice cream sandwiches, particularly for kids because of the cookies' small size.

8 ounces organic unsweetened chocolate

2 cups organic all—purpose flour

1/2 cup organic whole wheat pastry flour

3/4 cup organic unsweetened cocoa powder
   (I prefer Rapunzel brand)

1/2 teaspoon salt

1/2 teaspoon baking soda

2 sticks (1 cup) organic unsalted butter,
   softened

1 cup firmly packed organic dark—brown
   sugar

3 large organic eggs

2/3 cup organic white—chocolate chips

One 3.5 ounce bar dark chocolate, chopped
   into small pieces

1 cup chopped toasted organic walnuts

Preheat the oven to 350°F. Line 2 baking sheets with Silpats or parchment paper and set aside.

Melt the unsweetened chocolate in the top of a double boiler set over simmering water, or in short bursts in a microwave. Stir occasionally until the chocolate is melted. Remove from the heat and set aside.

In a medium bowl, sift the flours, cocoa powder, salt, and baking soda together. Set aside.

In a standing mixer fitted with the paddle attachment, cream the butter and brown sugar on medium speed until fluffy, about 3 minutes.

Add the eggs, one at a time, beating until well incorporated. Add the vanilla extract, melted chocolate, and 1 teaspoon water.

With the mixer on low speed, add the dry ingredients until just combined. Add the white-chocolate chips, chopped dark chocolate, and nuts.

Using a tablespoon-size ice cream scooper, place scoops of dough at least 2 inches apart on the prepared baking sheets.

Bake for 12 minutes. (It can be hard to tell when these cookies are done because they're dark in color, but they should be firm on the edges and still soft in the center.)

Let the cookies cool completely on the baking sheets. Then store them in an airtight container for up to 3 days.

TO MAKE ICE CREAM SANDWICHES

Cover a baking sheet with wax paper and line up 2 cookies for each sandwich.

Let vanilla or coffee ice cream sit out a little to soften. Use a small scooper or a tablespoon to scoop ice cream onto one cookie, top with the other cookie, and squish the cookies together a bit to help the ice cream fill any empty spots. Place the sandwiches in the freezer to harden.

After 10 minutes, you can wrap them in plastic wrap or store them in containers, so they won't smell like your freezer!

million-dollar cookies

Remember that funny Neiman Marcus cookie myth that went around in the eighties? A customer was said to have eaten one of Neiman Marcus's signature chocolate-chip cookies, asked for the recipe, and heard that it would cost "two fifty." Upon receiving the bill, the customer found she had been charged $250. Of course the story is pure urban legend, but Neiman Marcus was one of my mom's favorite stores, and she loved the Neiman Marcus cookie recipe. She always joked that since the cookies were worth $250, we could eat only a few at a time. Of course my brother, sister, and I found ways to swipe a dozen at a time before lapsing into a cookie coma while watching The Love Boat.

With interest, those cookies would now be worth a lot more than $250! I never stopped baking them, although I changed the recipe because I always found them too sweet and not chocolaty enough. I find them more flavorful than standard chocolate-chip cookies, although they do require a few extra steps to make them extra-delicious.

One 3.5—ounce bar organic dark
    chocolate, preferably Green & Black's
    70% baking chocolate, chilled
2 sticks (1 cup) organic unsalted butter,
    softened
1 ¼ cups Rapadura sugar (see page 14)
3 large organic eggs
1 teaspoon organic vanilla extract

1 teaspoon baking soda
1 cup organic whole wheat pastry flour
1 ½ cups oat flour (see Note)
1 teaspoon salt
12 ounces organic semisweet chocolate
    chips or Rapunzel 70% baking chips

Preheat the oven to 350°F. Line 2 baking sheets with Silpats or aluminum foil and set aside.

In a food processor, pulse the chilled chocolate bar until finely ground. (Having it chilled prevents it from melting from the heat of the blade.) Set aside.

In a standing mixer fitted with the whisk attachment, cream the butter and sugar on medium-high speed until light and fluffy, 3 to 5 minutes.

Add the eggs, one at a time, whisking until combined. Then add the vanilla, baking soda, and 1 teaspoon water.

Sift the whole wheat pastry flour into a medium bowl. Add the oat flour, salt, and the ground chocolate and whisk to combine. With the mixer on low speed, add the dry mixture to the butter-sugar mixture and combine thoroughly.

Using a rubber whisk, fold in the chocolate chips.

Wetting your hands with water, roll the dough into balls (about 1 tablespoon each), or use an ice cream scooper for less messy results. Place the balls 2 inches apart on the prepared baking sheets and bake for 10 minutes, or until golden brown on the edges.

Let the cookies cool on the baking sheets for a few minutes. Then transfer them to wire racks to cool completely.

Note: If you don't have oat flour on hand, simply grind small batches of rolled oats in a clean coffee grinder or a food processor until powdery.

crispy, chewy oatmeal raisin cookies

| MAKES 3 DOZEN COOKIES |

Three summers ago I went on an oatmeal-raisin baking binge. I had so many ideas for the perfect cookie, and I had to test them all out. I landed on this cookie: crisp, chewy, and delicate. Because it contains no flour, it won't puff up like cake or feel heavy. I made it in large batches whenever it was crunch time for our team when we were designing jewelry for Kenneth Cole and needed a boost to keep sketching late into the night. The cookies have crisp edges with a nice chew in the center, and if you make them large, they're a perfect treat on rainy summer days, with a dollop of vanilla ice cream on the side.

2 sticks (1 cup) organic unsalted butter, softened

1 cup firmly packed organic dark-brown sugar

1 cup organic cane sugar

2 large organic eggs

1 tablespoon organic vanilla extract

1 teaspoon baking powder

1 teaspoon baking soda

1 teaspoon salt

$1/2$ teaspoon organic ground cinnamon

$3 1/2$ cups organic rolled oats (not instant or quick-cooking)

$1/2$ cup organic toasted wheat germ

1 cup organic raisins or dried currants

1 cup chopped toasted organic walnuts or pecans (optional)

Preheat the oven to 350°F. Salivate with anticipation. Line 2 baking sheets with Silpats or parchment paper and set aside.

In the bowl of an electric mixer fitted with the paddle attachment, cream the butter and both sugars on medium-high speed until light and fluffy, about 3 minutes.

Add the eggs, one at a time, making sure to incorporate each one well before adding another. Mix in the vanilla extract.

In a separate bowl, sift the baking powder, baking soda, salt, and cinnamon together. Add this to the butter-sugar mixture, stirring until incorporated. Then, on low speed, add the oats, wheat germ, raisins, and walnuts (if using), stirring just until mixed.

Chill the dough until the butter firms up, about 30 minutes

Use a tablespoon-size ice cream scooper or a tablespoon to place balls of dough 5 inches apart on the prepared baking sheets. Bake 1 sheet at a time in the center of the oven for 16 to 18 minutes, or until the cookies are golden brown. They'll still be a little soft in the center, but this is the good, chewy part!

Cool the cookies on the baking sheets for 18 minutes. Then use a spatula to transfer them to wire racks to cool completely.

Ronnybrook makes perfect
cookie—dunking milk.

crisp, crumbly shortbread

This buttery, crisp shortbread can be flavored in so many ways: with herbs from the farm-ers' market (rosemary, lemon verbena, sage), with lavender, with crystallized ginger. After visiting a boutique in Paris that makes all its sweet and savory foods with infusions of tea, I was inspired to try flavoring the shortbread with a variety of tea leaves. For Ruby's first birthday tea party, I made it with an organic rose tea blend.

3 cups organic all—purpose flour
1 cup organic rice flour or cornstarch
1 teaspoon salt
4 sticks (2 cups) fresh farmers' market
    butter, softened (as this is the star
    ingredient, make it shine!)

1 cup organic cane sugar
1/4 cup minced fresh rosemary leaves (or
    see numerous fabulous alternatives
    below)

Sift the flour, rice flour or cornstarch, and salt together in a medium bowl and set aside.

In a standing mixer fitted with the paddle attachment or with a hand mixer, cream the butter on medium speed until light and fluffy, about 3 minutes. Slowly add the sugar, creaming for an additional 2 minutes until the mixture is even lighter and fluffier.

With the mixer running, slowly add the flour mixture. With the last bit of flour, add the rosemary or other flavoring. (Do not add the herbs or tea after the flour is completely mixed in, or it will over-work the dough.)

Lay a long piece of plastic wrap on your work surface.

FOR SLICED SHORTBREAD

Place the dough on the plastic wrap, shape it into a log, and wrap it well in the plastic wrap. Chill it in the refrigerator for at least 30 minutes before slicing.

When you are ready to slice the dough, preheat the oven to 375°F. Line 2 or more baking sheets with Silpats or parchment paper.

Cut the log of dough into $^{1}/_{4}$-inch-thick slices, arrange them 1 $^{1}/_{2}$ inches apart on the prepared baking sheets, and place the baking sheets in the freezer for 5 minutes.

FOR ROLLED SHORTBREAD

See page 101 to make perfect rolled cookies.

Place the dough on a sheet of parchment paper, or Silpat, with a sheet of parchment on top. Chill it in the refrigerator for at least 30 minutes.

When you are ready to roll out the dough, preheat the oven to 375°F.

Roll the dough to a $^{1}/_{2}$-inch thickness, sprinkling a little flour on the dough so it doesn't stick. I like to cut shapes out directly on the Silpat or parchment paper as the cookies can become misshapen if moved. To do this, cut out all your shapes, chill for 5 minutes, then peel away the excess dough surrounding the cookie cutouts and reuse. Arrange the cookies at least 1 inch apart on the prepared baking sheets.

Bake the shortbread, until golden, 18 to 20 minutes. (If you use 2 baking sheets on separate racks, the baking time will be shorter for the bottom sheet.)

Remove the baking sheets from the oven, let the shortbread sit for a few minutes, and transfer it to wire racks to cool.

flavor variations

Instead of the rosemary, add:

- EARL GREY Use the contents of 1 $1/2$ to 2 tea bags of organic Earl Grey tea. I like to add a few drops of black food coloring to make the cookies gray.

- ROSE Use the contents of 1 $1/2$ to 2 tea bags of organic rose tea. I add a few drops of red food coloring to make the cookies look pink and ladylike.

- MATCHA GREEN TEA Add 3 tablespoons organic matcha tea powder. The color will be a lovely shade of mint green.

- LAVENDER Use $1/4$ cup fresh farmers' market lavender or dried lavender flowers, and cut the dough with a flower-shaped cookie cutter.

- GINGER Add 3 tablespoons minced organic crystallized ginger. You can even add a few pinches of freshly ground black pepper to give it a real zing.

- A RAINBOW OF COLORS You can add food coloring to make any color to work with your party theme.

mexican-chocolate cookies

| MAKES 2 DOZEN COOKIES |

I was lucky enough to grow up close to Mexico, where I could taste authentic food made by friends' parents and at local taquerias. Mexican hot chocolate became a favorite drink, and my brother and I still always keep it on hand. Something about the blend of chocolate, cinnamon, and black pepper conquers my chocolate cravings instantly. I especially love drinking it in the winter, sitting by the window watching it snow outside.

Crisp, with a hint of spice, these treats are Mexican hot chocolate in a cookie. Cacao nibs add crunch and enhance the chocolate, cinnamon, and cayenne. Since the dough must be chilled before baking, you can either roll it out flat and use cookie cutters or, my personal preference, roll it into a log, then slice and bake. You can even whip up the dough quickly before guests arrive for dinner, and then chill it during your meal. As long as you preheat the oven about 10 minutes before dessert, you can slice, bake, and serve these cookies within 15 minutes. For holiday parties, I brush the chilled log with silver or gold dust before slicing to add a nice festive shimmer.

1 1/2 cups organic whole wheat pastry flour
3/4 cup organic unsweetened cocoa powder
1/4 teaspoon salt
Pinch of freshly ground black pepper
1/8 teaspoon cayenne pepper
3/4 teaspoon organic ground cinnamon
1 1/2 sticks (3/4 cup) organic unsalted butter, softened

1 cup firmly packed organic dark-brown sugar
1 organic egg
1 tablespoon organic vanilla extract
1/4 cup ground organic cacao nibs (see page 21)

Sift the flour, cocoa, salt, both peppers, and cinnamon together in a medium bowl.

Using a hand mixer or a standing mixer on medium speed, cream the butter for 3 minutes, or until pale and fluffy. Add the brown sugar, egg, and vanilla and mix to incorporate thoroughly.

With the mixer on low speed, add the dry ingredients, mixing until combined. Stir in the cacao nibs.

Shape the dough into a log, wrap it in plastic wrap, and place it in the freezer for 15 minutes. (If you want to make cutout cookies, pat the dough in a disk shape, wrap it in plastic wrap, and place it in the freezer.)

Meanwhile, preheat the oven to 375°F. Line a baking sheet with a Silpat or parchment paper.

Slice the dough into $^1/_4$-inch-thick disks and place them $1^1/_2$ inches apart on the prepared baking sheet. (If you are making cutout cookies, roll the dough on the Silpat or a very highly floured surface to a $^1/_4$-inch thickness, and use cookie cutters to cut them out.)

Bake for 8 to 9 minutes; the center will still be a little soft.

Remove the cookies immediately to a wire rack to cool completely.

Double ginger cookies may be the secret entrance to my husband's heart.

double ginger cookies

My friend Melissa McDonnell is finishing up her architectural studies in Texas, but she always finds time to bake her famous ginger cookies.

These cookies are chewy, hearty, and totally addictive. The dough does need to chill for an hour, so be sure to prepare accordingly. And keep a close eye on these—my husband is a ginger-cookie addict and stole almost half the batch while they were cooling.

There's one catch to these cookies, which you can read about at the bottom of page 120. Don't let it deter you from baking them!

1 1/2 cups organic all—purpose flour

1 1/2 cups organic whole wheat flour

1 teaspoon baking powder

1/2 teaspoon baking soda

1/2 teaspoon salt

1 teaspoon organic ground ginger

3/4 cup minced organic crystallized ginger

1 1/4 cups organic cane sugar

2 tablespoons organic ground flaxseed

1/2 cup organic unsweetened applesauce (see Note)

1/4 cup organic canola oil

1 teaspoon grated organic lemon zest

1 tablespoon fresh organic lemon juice

1/2 teaspoon organic vanilla extract

In a large bowl, whisk together the flours, baking powder, baking soda, salt, ground ginger, and crystallized ginger.

In a separate bowl, combine I cup of the sugar and all the remaining ingredients.

Stir the two mixtures together until moist and incorporated, shape into a disk, and cover with plastic wrap. Cover and refrigerate for I hour, or up to I day.

Preheat the oven to 350°F. Place the remaining 1/4 cup sugar in a shallow bowl. Use 2 Silpats or lightly grease 2 cookie sheets.

Flour your hands and form the dough into 1-inch balls. Roll the dough balls through the sugar, and then flatten them with the greased bottom of a drinking glass or cup. Place the cookies 2 inches apart on the prepared baking sheets.

Bake the cookies for 18 minutes, or until slightly browned (they won't get very dark, so be careful not to keep them in too long).

Let the cookies cool on the baking sheets for a minute. Then transfer them to wire racks to cool completely.

Note: Tip for parents: Snack packs of applesauce come in $^1/_2$-cup servings.

Secret: These cookies are vegan, but you'd never know the difference!

salty and sweet peanut butter cookies

| MAKES 2 DOZEN COOKIES |

These peanut butter cookies have tons of personality and satisfy all the taste buds—making it hard to just eat one. When I was growing up, my grandma and I always made them together. They are thin, crisp-edged cookies with a chewy center, and they're sprinkled with chopped peanuts and a pinch of salt to ensure that each bite has the perfect balance of sweet, salty, and peanuty. I like to use fancy black salt on top that I find at Trader Joe's to give these cookies a super-chic touch.

1 stick ($1/2$ cup) organic unsalted butter, softened

1 cup organic smooth peanut butter (see page 22)

$1/2$ cup organic cane sugar

$3/4$ cup firmly packed organic dark-brown sugar

1 large organic egg

1 teaspoon sea salt

1 tablespoon organic vanilla extract

1 cup organic all-purpose flour

$3/4$ teaspoon baking soda

1 cup crushed roasted salted organic peanuts

Black Himalayan salt or Maldon brand sea salt flakes, for sprinkling

Preheat the oven to 350°F. Line 2 baking sheets with Silpats or parchment paper and set aside.

In the bowl of an electric mixer fitted with the paddle attachment, cream the butter, peanut butter, salt, and sugars together on medium-high speed until light and fluffy, 3 to 4 minutes. Add the egg and vanilla and mix on medium speed until well combined.

In a medium mixing bowl, sift the flour and baking soda together. Add this dry mixture to the butter mixture and beat just to combine. Add the salted peanuts, reserving 2 tablespoons for sprinkling on top, and beat just until combined.

Scooping out the dough with 2 tablespoons, shape the dough into balls and place them 3 inches apart on the prepared baking sheets. Dip the tines of a fork in warm water and press the dough balls lightly with the back of the fork to flatten them slightly (dip the fork back in the water for each dough ball, to prevent sticking). Sprinkle each cookie with the remaining crushed nuts and a few grains of Himalayan or Maldon sea salt.

Bake, rotating the baking sheets between the oven shelves halfway through baking, until golden brown, 18 to 20 minutes.

Transfer the baking sheets to a wire rack to cool. Store the cookies in an airtight container for up to 1 week.

Black sea salt makes these cookies
stand out on the plate.

Dust gold and silver dust on brownies to make a shiny impact (see page 238).

one-bowl dark gooey brownies

| MAKES ABOUT 2 DOZEN SMALL GOOEY BROWNIES |

My friend Carolyn opened a boutique named after her children, Jan and Aya, in Green-point last spring. For the opening party, I baked these brownies, dusted them with gold dust, and cut them into bite-size squares. Carolyn placed platters of them all over the store and they were gone within an hour! People still talk about how gooey and dark-chocolaty they were. Little did they know I use only a small amount of whole wheat flour and mix everything in one bowl! They're simple to make and require little cleanup. I like to be resourceful and eco-friendly by covering the bottom of the brownie pan with butter wrappers, butter side up. (Save butter wrappers by placing them in a plastic freezer bag whenever you go through butter sticks. Simply defrost when you're preparing your pan.)

For a gorgeous—and easy—presentation, brush these brownies with metallic gold powder, or mix both silver and gold for a glittery effect.

1 1/2 sticks (3/4 cup) organic butter

8 ounces organic semisweet chocolate

8 ounces organic unsweetened chocolate, softened

2 cups organic cane sugar

4 organic eggs

2 heaping teaspoons organic free-trade instant decaffeinated coffee

1 tablespoon organic vanilla extract

3/4 cup organic whole wheat pastry flour

1 cup chopped organic walnuts (optional)

Silver and/or gold metallic dust (see page 238) or powdered sugar, for dusting (optional)

Preheat the oven to 350°F. Place butter wrappers, butter side up, on the bottom of a 9 x 13-inch baking pan, or simply butter the pan. (If the wrappers don't cover the entire pan, you can easily cover the extra space with parchment paper.) Set aside.

Melt the butter and chocolate in the top of a double boiler set over simmering water, or with short bursts in a microwave, until mostly melted. Then let the mixture stand until the remaining pieces of chocolate are melted. Pour the mixture into a large bowl.

Mix in the sugar and then the eggs, one at a time. Dissolve the instant coffee in 1 teaspoon hot water. Add the coffee and vanilla to the mixture and mix thoroughly. Add the flour and whisk until combined. The mixture should be thick.

Add the walnuts (if using) and pour the batter into the prepared baking pan, scraping the sides of the bowl with a rubber spatula. Smooth the top evenly.

Bake the brownies for 20 to 22 minutes, or until slightly firm to the touch.

Let the brownies cool in the pan on a wire rack until warm; then place the pan in the refrigerator for at least 2 hours to set.

When you are ready to cut them, use a knife dipped in hot water, wiped clean, to cut the brownies into small squares. If you like, brush on gold or silver metallic powder for an elegant effect, or dust lightly with powdered sugar.

Store in an airtight container in the refrigerator for up to 1 week.

lemon-lime bars

Meyer lemons do make the best lemon bars, but usually my bootleg supply from my trips to California runs out pretty quickly. Occasionally I can find them at the supermarket. I like to add lime to my lemon bars, to give them a little more pucker, and I use whole wheat flour to make the crust nutty and crisp, like a shortbread.

FOR THE CRUST

4 sticks (2 cups) organic unsalted butter, softened

$1/2$ cup organic powdered sugar, plus more for garnish

1 cup organic whole wheat pastry flour

$1/2$ cup organic wheat germ

$1/2$ teaspoon salt

FOR THE LEMON—LIME FILLING

7 large organic eggs

$3/4$ cup plus 2 tablespoons organic all—purpose flour

$3^1/2$ cups organic cane sugar

$1/2$ cup fresh organic lemon juice

$1/2$ cup fresh organic lime juice

1 tablespoon grated organic lemon zest

1 tablespoon grated organic lime zest

FOR THE TOPPING

Sifted powdered sugar

Candied Lemon or Lime Slices (page 74, optional)

In an electric mixer or a standing mixer fitted with the whisk attachment, cream the butter and powdered sugar on medium speed until fluffy, around 3 minutes. Add the flour, wheat germ, and salt, and beat until combined. Press the dough into a 9 x 13-inch baking pan, distributing it evenly and making sure you cover the sides of the pan as well as the bottom. Let chill in the refrigerator while you preheat the oven to 350°F.

Bake for 15 to 20 minutes, or until the crust is light brown and set. Let cool completely.

Meanwhile, whisk all the filling ingredients together in a medium bowl.

Pour the filling into the cooled crust and bake for 25 to 30 minutes, or until the filling is set.

Sprinkle the bars with sifted powdered sugar, and decorate them with Candied Lemon or Lime Slices if desired.

Chill until cold and slice the bars using a knife dipped in hot water.

Place the cut bars on a stacked serving tray or on a plate.

grandma eva's mandelbrot

| MAKES 3 DOZEN PIECES |

My grandma Eva, one of my fashion heroes, always sported red-painted nails, chunky costume jewelry, and rhinestone-studded glasses. A jazz singer, she owned a collection of records that got a kitchen dance party going, with Hawaiian fire-eater music, big band tunes, and jazz greats. She looked after us frequently when we were young and would bake this Jewish version of biscotti whenever she came over. The recipe changed according to what we had lying around in the pantry, including chocolate chips, nuts, raisins, or dried fruits, but her specialty was toasted coconut and pecan.

2 $1/4$ cups organic all-purpose flour
1 cup organic whole wheat pastry flour
1 teaspoon baking powder
1 cup organic cane sugar
$1/2$ teaspoon salt
Pinch of organic ground cinnamon
3 organic eggs
2 teaspoons organic vanilla extract
1 cup organic canola oil

One or 2 of the following add-ins: 1 cup organic chocolate chips, $3/4$ cup chopped toasted organic nuts (almonds, pecans, pistachios, hazelnuts, pumpkin seeds, or a combination), $1/2$ cup shredded toasted organic unsweetened coconut, $1/2$ cup organic raisins or other chopped organic dried fruit

Preheat the oven to 350°F. Line a baking sheet with a piece of aluminum foil, oil the foil lightly, and set aside.

In a large bowl, whisk the flours, baking powder, sugar, salt, and cinnamon together.

Whisk the eggs, vanilla, and oil together in a smaller bowl.

Make a well in the center of the dry ingredients, pour in the wet ingredients, and whisk until just combined. Throw in your customized add-ins.

Place the dough on the oiled aluminum foil, shaping it into a loaf with your hands.

Bake until light brown, about 30 minutes. Remove from the oven, but keep the oven on.

Let the loaf cool slightly on the baking sheet. When it's cool enough to handle, use a serrated knife to cut the loaf into $1/2$-inch-thick slices.

Lay each piece flat on the baking sheet. (You may need to cover an additional baking sheet with oiled foil.) Bake for 10 minutes, or until the cookies are light brown. Let cool on the baking sheet.

Store in an airtight container for up to 1 week or freeze, as desired.

Note: My grandma used to melt any remaining chocolate from the bag of chocolate chips and drizzle it over the mandelbrot. You can also make a version without any chocolate chips and then melt a bag of chocolate chips, dip one end of each mandelbrot in the chocolate, and let them cool on wax paper.

Grandma Eva with her crazy white hat

reformed junk food

LET'S NOT FOOL OURSELVES. Just because we love organic and healthy food doesn't mean there aren't those times when we just want to eat candy bars and junk food.

When my son was three years old, we visited a huge grocery store where we don't usually shop. I pushed him in the cart, past the aisle where the shelves were piled high with boxes of Twinkies, Ding Dongs, and Yodels. Seeing the pictures of a Twinkie, he asked me to buy a box. I could understand why he wanted it: the Twinkie on the box looked so creamy and delicious. Once I read the ingredients, however, I told him, "No way, José. I don't even understand what this is made out of! We'll make something better at home."

That night I was on a mission to re-create that creamy Twinkie, but to make one that tasted as good as that picture looked. Of course I knew that whatever I would bake would taste better because it would be made with fresh, organic ingredients and no hydrogenated oils. Not only did my son chomp them down, my husband did too, and so have hundreds of friends, clients, and coworkers.

As adults, we crave the sweets of our childhood. We grow up and start to eat good food, and when we try to enjoy flavors from the past, they may not taste exactly the way we remembered them. Making junk food healthful has been important for me. I want to build a new frame of reference for Clyde and Ruby, so that when they're older, they'll reminisce about my homemade sweets rather than about packaged junk food. After all, if your mom knew what we know now about the ingredients in those kinds of sweets, she probably wouldn't have let you near them!

Clyde and Ruby

goldies

Goldies, my organic twist on a Twinkie, have become one of my most notorious treats. I like to bake these with the Easiest Chocolate Cake (page 43) as a base, as it's the perfect partner to the sweet, creamy filling and dark, almost bittersweet ganache. For a chic finish, I brush them with gold metallic dust.

To give the Goldies their unique look, you will need specialty baking pans. These pans are commonly sold as éclair pans, but since éclairs went out of style two decades ago, you may have better luck ordering them (and the wrappers if you want) online through cooking-supply stores such as www.kitchenkrafts.com, www.sugarcraft.com, or www.cakedeco.com.

Organic unsweetened cocoa powder, for
   dusting the pans
Batter for Easiest Chocolate Cake
   (page 43)
Vanilla or Espresso Whipped Buttercream
   (pages 84, 85)

Melted Chocolate Ganache (recipe follows)
Gold metallic powder (see page 238), for
   dusting

Preheat the oven to 350°F. Spray 2 éclair pans with organic cooking spray and dust them with cocoa powder; set aside. Fit a small pastry bag with a size-12 tip and set aside.

Using a ladle, fill each prepared éclair mold two-thirds full with cake batter. Bake for exactly 18 minutes. A cake tester should come out clean.

Let the cake sit in the pans for 5 to 10 minutes. Then hold each pan upside down and gently coax the Goldies out. Place them upside down on a wire rack and allow to cool completely.

Once they have cooled, use a serrated knife to trim off the domed excess cake on the bottom of each Goldie. Eat the scraps as a reward for your hard work, but be careful: they're addictive!

Fill the pastry bag with buttercream. One at a time, turn the cakes over and starting at one end, insert the piping tip almost an inch deep and insert a bit of cream. Do this every $\frac{1}{2}$ inch. You should end up with 3 or 4 holes in the bottom of each Goldie where you've inserted the buttercream. (My motto is "A bite of cream in every bite!") When all the Goldies are filled, cover them with plastic wrap and chill in the refrigerator for at least 15 minutes.

While the Goldies are chilling, prepare the Melted Chocolate Ganache. As it cools, set up a work area by covering a baking sheet with parchment paper.

Éclair pans give Goldies the perfect shape.

Insert the piping tip every $\frac{1}{2}$ inch.

One at a time, with the rounded side facing down, dip the Goldies halfway into the ganache. Flip them over and place them upright on the parchment paper. Use a small spatula to spread the chocolate over all sides of the Goldies except the bottom. Once they are coated, return the Goldies to the refrigerator to allow the coating to set, about 20 minutes.

Place the Goldies on a serving tray or in individual éclair wrappers. Using a 1-inch brush, lightly brush gold metallic powder on top of the Goldies, going back and forth to ensure they're covered completely in gold.

Spread the ganache with a small offset spatula.

Once chilled, dust with gold metallic powder.

melted chocolate ganache

Let the ganache cool to lukewarm before you use it. If it's too hot, it will simply absorb into the cake and disappear.

| MAKES ABOUT 2¹/₂ CUPS |

1 stick (¹/₂ cup) organic unsalted butter
Two 7—ounce bars organic 70% baking
   chocolate (or for real dark—chocolate
   lovers, use unsweetened chocolate)

2 cups organic semisweet chocolate
   chips

Place the butter and chocolate in the top of a double boiler or in a stainless-steel bowl placed over a saucepan one-quarter full of water. Over medium-high heat, stir the mixture frequently with a rubber spatula until the chocolate is almost melted. Remove from the bottom pan and stir until the chocolate has finished melting.

Cool for 15 minutes or more, until thickened, before using.

to decorate |

BESIDES DUSTING THE GANACHE WITH METALLIC POWDER, you can simply drizzle melted white chocolate on top of the dark ganache for contrast; or after coating the Goldies with the ganache, freeze them for 10 minutes and then dip them halfway in warm melted white chocolate—a twist on the black and white cookie.

silver ring-a-dings

| MAKES 24 CUPCAKES |

These are the perfect companion to any dessert table that showcases "reformed" junk food. I like to decorate these with a brush of silver metallic powder instead of the familiar white frosting squiggle. Use gold cupcake liners, or to be more eco-chic, use recycled brown liners. For a chocolate-mint cupcake, use peppermint extract instead of vanilla when you make the Vanilla Whipped Buttercream. Or (my favorite) substitute orange extract for the vanilla.

Butter for Easiest Chocolate Cake
   (page 43)
Vanilla Whipped Buttercream (page 84)

Melted Chocolate Ganache (page 140)
Silver metallic powder (see page 238)

Preheat the oven to 350°F. Place liners in two 12-cup muffin pans and set aside. Fit a small pastry bag with a size-12 tip and set it aside.

Fill the muffin cups two-thirds full with the cake butter. Bake for 16 to 18 minutes, or until a cake tester inserted in the center comes out clean.

Set the cupcakes aside to cool on a wire rack, then remove the cupcakes. The cupcakes must be at room temperature before filling. (You can bake these earlier in the day or the day before; just wrap them well in plastic wrap and leave them on your work surface or refrigerate them.)

Fill the pastry bag with buttercream. Use a size-12 tip. Holding the bag at a 90-degree angle, insert the tip almost an inch into each cupcake, and apply pressure to fill the center. (You should see a slight swelling. This is the sign that you're making an excellent Ring-a-Ding!)

Insert the piping tip into the center.

Apply pressure, then release.

Chill the cupcakes in the refrigerator to set the filling, about 15 minutes.

Prepare the Melted Chocolate Ganache and allow it to cool.

Using a small spatula, frost the cupcakes with the ganache. Chill for about 15 minutes to set the ganache.

Once the cupcakes have chilled, brush them with silver metallic powder.

The yummy, creamy center

chocolate cream sandwiches

| MAKES 2 DOZEN COOKIES |

This is a delightful, not-too-sweet version of Oreos that I love to give as a housewarming present. If I'm feeling particularly kooky, I'll add flavoring to the cream filling, such as peppermint or even a tablespoon of espresso powder. It gives the cookies a new attitude and makes them irresistible. I rarely use shortening for baking, but it's the only thing I've found that will give this filling its rich, sugary, thick consistency. Spectrum is the only company that offers organic shortening.

FOR THE COOKIES

2 sticks (1 cup) organic unsalted butter, softened

2 cups organic cane sugar

2 organic eggs

1 1/2 tablespoons organic vanilla extract

2 cups organic unsweetened cocoa powder

1 cup organic whole wheat pastry flour

FOR THE CREAM FILLING

4 cups organic powdered sugar

1 teaspoon organic vanilla extract (see Note)

1/2 cup Spectrum organic shortening

Line 2 baking sheets with parchment paper, and cut 2 more sheets of parchment the same size. Set aside.

In a standing mixer fitted with the paddle attachment, cream the butter and sugar on medium speed until fluffy, 3 to 5 minutes. Add the eggs, one at a time, mixing until combined. Add the vanilla.

In a small bowl, sift the cocoa powder and flour together.

With the mixer on low speed, add the flour mixture until combined. You may want to finish mixing by hand with a rubber spatula, scraping down the sides of the bowl.

Divide the mixture in half, and place each half on a parchment-lined baking sheet. Lay the other sheets of parchment on top. Using a rolling pin, roll the dough to a $1/8$-inch thickness.

Chill the dough on the baking sheets in the refrigerator for 30 minutes, or until firm.

Meanwhile, preheat the oven to 350°F.

Working with 1 sheet of dough at a time, use a small drinking glass or a 2-inch round cutter to cut out the cookies. (Sometimes I use heart-shaped cutters for engagement parties—or just for kicks!)

Peel away the excess cookie dough, reshape it into a disk, and repeat the steps for rolling and cutting. (Be sure to make an even number of cookies.)

Space the cookies at least $1/2$ inch apart on the parchment-lined baking sheets, and bake for 8 to 10 minutes.

Let the cookies cool for a few minutes on the sheets, and then use a spatula to transfer them to a wire rack to cool completely.

While they are cooling, make the cream filling: In a standing mixer fitted with the whisk attachment, or with a hand mixer, combine all the filling ingredients on low speed. Increase the speed as the ingredients begin to incorporate. The filling should be thick and pasty.

Scoop up $1/2$ tablespoon of the filling and place it on the bottom of a cooled cookie. Then cover the filling with another cooled cookie, pressing down lightly to form a sandwich. Repeat to fill all the cookies. Store the cookies in an airtight container for up to 2 days, or keep them, well wrapped, in the refrigerator for up to 1 week.

Note: If you like, substitute 1 teaspoon peppermint, almond, or orange extract, or 1 teaspoon instant espresso powder dissolved in 1 tablespoon boiling water, for the vanilla.

For Double-Dipped Sandwiches

It's fun to coat these cookies partly or wholly with chocolate.

12 ounces organic semisweet chocolate chips or white—chocolate chips

Chill the filled cookies in the refrigerator for at least 30 minutes.

Place a wire rack on top of a sheet of wax paper.

Melt the chocolate chips in the top of a double boiler set over simmering water, or in short bursts in a microwave.

Using a fork or a spatula, dip each cookie halfway or entirely in the melted chocolate.

Let the cookies cool on the wire rack. Store between sheets of wax paper in an airtight container in the refrigerator for up to 1 week.

skinny mints

Thin Mints defined my childhood. We would buy so many boxes of Girl Scout cookies that we had to freeze half of them to avoid eating them too quickly. Of course the last box was a prized possession, and my parents had to ration it out among my siblings and me. We bartered the best stickers from our prized sticker collections for the last few cookies. In those days, the cookies came around only once a year. My version tastes better, because the chocolate coating is thick and tends to melt onto your hands (because it doesn't have preservatives in it). Keep them in the fridge or the freezer, and make sure your hands are clean so that you can keep licking off the chocolate!

1 1/4 cups organic unsweetened cocoa powder

2 3/4 cups organic all—purpose flour

1/2 teaspoon salt

2 sticks (1 cup) organic unsalted butter

2 cups organic powdered sugar

1/2 cup organic firmly packed dark—brown sugar

2 large organic eggs

1 tablespoon organic vanilla extract

Mint Glaze (recipe follows)

Line 2 baking sheets with parchment paper, and cut 2 more sheets of parchment the same size. Set aside.

In a medium bowl, sift together the cocoa powder, flour, and salt. Set aside.

In a standing mixer or with a hand mixer, cream the butter and sugars on medium speed until pale and fluffy, around 3 minutes. On low speed, add the eggs, one at a time, and the vanilla, and beat until combined.

Keeping the mixer on low speed, slowly add the dry ingredients just until combined, scraping down the sides of the bowl to ensure that they're mixed evenly.

Using your fingers or a spatula, scrape the dough to the center of the bowl, forming a mound. Divide the dough in half and place each half on a parchment-lined baking sheet. Lay the other sheets of parchment on top. Use a rolling pin to roll each piece of dough to around a $1/2$-inch thickness.

Chill the dough on the baking sheets in the refrigerator for 10 to 15 minutes.

Working with one sheet of dough at a time, roll the dough out to a $1/4$-inch thickness. Remove the top sheet of wax paper and choose your cookie shape. For ease, I use the mouth of a small drinking glass as a round cookie cutter, but you can use all kinds of shapes for these; hearts for Valentine's Day, candy canes for Christmas, four-leaf clovers for St. Patrick's Day, or my personal favorite, different sizes of stars for Hanukkah parties. Cut out the cookies and lay them $1/2$ inch apart on the parchment. Reroll the scraps of dough and repeat the rolling and cutting.

Place the baking sheets in the refrigerator for 10 minutes to chill the dough.

Meanwhile, preheat the oven to 350°F.

Bake the cookies until firm, around 12 minutes. (It's hard to tell when chocolate cookies are done, as you cannot see them brown, but don't overbake them or they'll become too crisp.)

Remove the cookies from the oven and let them cool completely on wire racks.

Cover your work surface with wax paper or aluminum foil. Using a spatula or a fork, dip each cookie into the warm mint-chocolate glaze, coating both sides and letting the excess drip off before placing the cookie on the wax paper. For a cleaner—and more chic—look, dip only half the cookie.

Store the cookies in between sheets of wax paper in an airtight container in the refrigerator for up to 1 week.

mint glaze

This glaze is minty and chocolaty and thickens as it cools. If you're crazy about mint, add a touch more peppermint extract.

| MAKES ABOUT 2 CUPS |

12 ounces organic semisweet chocolate chips
1 stick (½ cup) organic unsalted butter, softened

1 tablespoon organic peppermint extract

Melt the chocolate and butter in the top of a double boiler set over simmering water, stirring frequently. Remove the top pan from the heat when the chocolate is almost completely melted, and stir in the peppermint extract.

Use while still warm.

black-and-white skinny mints

I like to make this version for more sophisticated events, like engagement parties, foodie-mom baby showers, and anniversary parties.

6 ounces organic white-chocolate chips

2 sticks (1 cup) organic unsalted butter

1 teaspoon organic peppermint extract

6 ounces organic semisweet chocolate chips

You'll need two double boilers or two microwave-safe bowls to make these pretty cookies. In one double boiler, melt the white chocolate chips, 1 stick of the butter, and 1/2 teaspoon of the peppermint extract. In the other, melt the semisweet chocolate chips, the remaining 1 stick butter, and the remaining 1/2 teaspoon peppermint extract. Taste both glazes to make sure they have enough peppermint kick in them.

Dip each a cookie halfway into the white chocolate mixture. Chill the cookies in the refrigerator for 10 minutes, and then dip the other side in the semisweet chocolate mixture.

snowballz

I love to serve these fluffy, creamy coconut creations in the springtime. Something about them reminds me of bunnies, fluffy clouds, and dreamy thoughts in the sunshine. When I'm feeling particularly health-conscious, I use unsweetened coconut, and if I'm channeling Martha, I cut chunks of fresh coconut.

Depending on the coconut you use and your preference, you can create giant, chunky coconut snowballs or keep them dainty and petite, and you can use almost any cake inside (see below for suggestions). For delightful little treats that look like pom-poms, use a mini-cupcake pan.

1 recipe Vanilla–Bean Butter Cake
    (page 37), Easiest Chocolate Cake
    (page 43), or Coco Loco (page 48)
1 recipe Classic Americana Icing (page 86)

1 pound dried shredded organic coconut,
    sweetened or unsweetened
Food coloring (for the coconut)

Follow the recipe for your choice of cake, making either traditional cupcakes or mini cupcakes.

While the cupcakes are baking, prepare the Classic Americana Icing, using the vanilla extract or almond, peppermint, or orange extract (see Note).

Once the cupcakes have cooled, remove them from the liners and trim the edges on top so each cupcake looks rounded, almost like a ball. Snack on the trimmings.

Fit a small pastry bag with a size-12 tip and fill the bag with icing. Insert the tip almost all the way into the center of each cupcake, pressing gently to release some frosting inside the cupcake.

Line 2 baking sheets with parchment paper and set them aside. Tape a large piece of parchment paper on a clean work surface.

In a large plastic bag that zips shut, combine 2 cups of the coconut and a few drops of food coloring. Use a separate bag for each color. Close the bag and shake to distribute the color evenly. Spread the colored coconut flakes in an even layer on the taped-down parchment paper.

Working with only a few cupcakes at a time, frost the cupcakes all over with the remaining icing, and then roll them in the coconut flakes to cover all the icing.

Place the Snowballz on a baking sheet lined with parchment paper, and chill in the refrigerator until the icing is set, about 10 minutes. Cover them well with plastic wrap, so they don't absorb refrigerator smells, and store in the refrigerator.

Note: You can also divide the icing in half and prepare two different flavors. This is especially chic if you also mix up the cake flavors, making half of your cupcake batch chocolate and half vanilla.

farmers' market
sweets

fall harvest

Every Saturday (except in a blizzard or when it's too cold to get out of bed), my family gets up, purposely forgets to shower, and walks the few blocks to our local farmers' market. Usually it's buzzing with activity, earthy smells, bugs and bees, sunshine, and the friends and kids that make up our small community in Brooklyn. As we enter the market, the heavenly scent of freshly picked fruits and vegetables perfumes the air. A local jazz group sits on old wooden crates and plays bebop music for the kids to dance to. As we wait in line for the "meat man," we chat with friends and new neighbors about kids and recipes.

The weekly frenzy seems like a distant memory. Coming into contact with local farmers evokes an era that has become divorced from the urban landscape. At each farm stand, the purveyors offer helpful suggestions about which produce is fresh to the season and relate any other interesting news about produce. While my husband takes Clyde to the playground across the street, Ruby and I wander to each stand, asking about what's just been picked and what's tasting especially good and sampling the local fare.

There's nothing that says spring and summer to me more than setting up a picnic in the park with freshly baked farmers' market sweets. Fresh fruit and vegetables taste different than those found in the grocery store. Usually they've been picked within a day of the market and are crisper, fresher, and more earthy, with depth and color unlike any commercially grown produce.

fall pear and ginger tart

| MAKES ONE 10−INCH TART OR FIVE 4−INCH TARTLETS |

You can taste all the hues of autumn in this rustic, crisp, and spicy tart. The flavors of both crystallized and fresh ginger come together with ripe pears for an impressive but easy dessert. Prepare it either in a 10-inch tart shell or in mini tartlets for serving at larger parties or dinners.

FOR THE CRUST

1 cup organic whole wheat pastry flour

1 3/4 cup organic all−purpose flour

1 cup firmly packed Rapadura (see page 14)
   or organic dark−brown sugar

3 tablespoons minced organic crystallized
   ginger

1 cup ground organic pecans (see Note)

1/2 teaspoon salt

2 sticks organic unsalted butter, chilled
   and cut into small pieces

1 organic egg yolk

1 tablespoon organic vanilla extract

FOR THE PEAR FILLING

2 pounds (9 or 10) ripe, farm−fresh
   Bartlett or D'Anjou pears, peeled,
   cored, and sliced into 1/4−inch−thick
   pieces

1/4 cup firmly packed organic dark−brown
   sugar or Rapadura sugar

2 teaspoons grated organic lemon zest

2 tablespoons freshly squeezed organic
   lemon juice

3 tablespoons freshly grated ginger

1/2 teaspoon cinnamon

2 tablespoons all−purpose flour

1 tablespoon vanilla extract

FOR SERVING

Vanilla Whipped Cream (page 180)

Note: I clean out my coffee grinder and blitz the nuts in small batches. Just be careful not to overgrind—you'll end up with nut butter!

TO PREPARE THE CRUST

In a food processor, combine the flours, sugar, crystallized ginger, pecans, and salt and pulse for 10 seconds. Add the cubes of chilled butter, a few at a time, pulsing on and off for 1 minute, until the mixture looks like bread crumbs.

Add the egg yolk and vanilla, pulsing on and off until the mixture is combined.

Press 2 cups of the mixture into the bottom and sides of the tart pan. Reserve the remaining crust dough for the top of the tart.

Preheat the oven to 375°F.

FOR THE FILLING

In a medium bowl, mix the pears, sugar, lemon zest, lemon juice, and ginger.

Add the remaining ingredients, mixing with a spatula to coat the pears evenly.

TO ASSEMBLE THE TART

Arrange the pears in an attractive even layer in the crust and pour the remaining liquid on top.

Remove the extra crust dough from the refrigerator and crumble evenly on top.

Place the tart on a baking sheet lined with foil and bake for 50 to 55 minutes, or until golden brown.

Let cool on a wire rack and serve warm with the whipped cream.

ginny tapper's fuji apple tart

| MAKES ONE 9-INCH TART |

This recipe marries a little bit of Wisconsin with a little bit of Tokyo via my friend Matthew Congdon, a sweater designer for the Japanese brand Uniqlo. We met almost eight years ago, when I was designing shoes and he was designing sweaters at J. Crew, and we've been friends ever since. An excellent baker, Matthew is the only person I know who can carry on a forty-five minute conversation about red-velvet cake and the latest macaroon flavors sold in the 7-Eleven store in Tokyo. He's a world traveler and a sweet-toothed foodie, trying all kinds of experimental treats and telling me about them in detail.

Matthew started baking as a baby with his grandma, Virginia Tapper, who lived in Wisconsin. At her recent funeral, a picture was displayed of Matthew at four years old, holding a pumpkin pie with Virginia in her kitchen. In honor of her and the love of baking she instilled in him, Matthew shares with us her apple tart, which he's updated here with organic Fuji apples from upstate New York.

Although the recipe looks as if it takes hours to make, it's actually quick and easy. (Matthew sometimes even bakes two at a time, bringing one in to work to make his co-workers swoon.)

FOR THE CRUST

¹/₂ stick (¹/₄ cup) organic unsalted butter,
   softened

¹/₃ cup organic cane sugar

¹/₂ teaspoon organic vanilla extract

³/₄ cup organic all-purpose flour

¹/₄ cup organic almond flour (ground
   almonds without the skins)

FOR THE CUSTARD FILLING

8 ounces organic cream cheese, softened

¹/₄ cup organic cane sugar

1 organic egg, lightly beaten

¹/₂ teaspoon organic vanilla extract

FOR THE APPLE TOPPING

3 or 4 medium organic Fuji apples

¹/₄ cup organic cane sugar

¹/₂ teaspoon organic ground
   cinnamon

FOR THE GLAZE

2 tablespoons orange marmalade

1 teaspoon brandy

Preheat the oven to 370°F. Butter the bottom and sides of a
9-inch tart pan with a removable bottom and set aside.

In a standing mixer fitted with the paddle attachment, cream the
butter and sugar together on medium speed, about 3 minutes. Add
the vanilla.

Add the flours to the butter mixture, and mix on low speed until
combined.

Transfer the mixture to the prepared tart pan and press in evenly
over the bottom and sides.

Make the custard filling: In a standing mixer fitted with the whisk
attachment, mix the cream cheese and sugar on medium speed until
smooth, 3 to 5 minutes. Add the egg and vanilla, and mix until

smooth, scraping down the sides of the bowl. Pour the filling into the tart shell.

Make the apple topping: Peel, core, and finely slice the apples. (I like to slice the apples by hand, but Matthew's grandma admitted to using a mandoline.) Toss in a bowl with the sugar and cinnamon.

Arrange the apple slices in a single overlapping layer around the outer edge of the tart. Then make an apple rose center by arranging slices, on their edges, in the custard, overlapping, in a circle until completely filled in (see page 160).

Bake the tart for 45 to 55 minutes, or until the filling has puffed up and the apples' edges have browned. Let cool.

Melt the marmalade with the brandy in a saucepan over medium heat, stirring until smooth. Strain the mixture into a small bowl, and apply it to the apples with a pastry brush.

Store the tart, well wrapped, in the refrigerator. Allow it to come to room temperature for serving.

To serve, carefully remove the sides of the tart pan and place the tart on an elegant serving plate.

plum galette

| MAKES 4 MINI GALETTES OR 1 LARGE GALETTE |

Ripe Italian plums are one of my favorite fruits to bake with at the end of the summer, especially because they become sweeter and buttery when baked in these galettes. Mix in some nectarines or peaches with the plums for a stone-fruit extravaganza, perfect for a casual dinner party with a few friends.

FOR THE PASTRY

$1/2$ cup organic whole wheat pastry flour

$3/4$ cup organic all-purpose flour

$1/2$ cup organic cane sugar, plus more for sprinkling

$3/4$ teaspoon salt

$1 \, 3/4$ sticks organic unsalted butter, chilled and cut into small pieces

1 teaspoon organic vanilla extract

2 teaspoons fresh organic lemon juice

FOR THE PLUM FILLING

1 pound ripe farm-fresh organic Italian plums (15 to 17 plums), cut into quarters, pits removed

2 tablespoons organic unsalted butter, softened

1 tablespoon firmly packed organic dark-brown sugar

Preheat the oven to 400°F. Line a baking sheet with parchment paper and set aside.

Combine the flours, sugar, and salt in a food processor and pulse for a few seconds. With the machine on low speed, add the chilled butter, one piece at a time, until the dough resembles a coarse meal.

Add the vanilla extract and lemon juice, pulsing on and off until the dough becomes wet and sticks together when you pinch it.

Remove the dough from the machine and shape it into either 4 disks or 1 large disk, both about $^1/_4$ inch thick. Wrap the disk(s) in plastic wrap and refrigerate for 30 minutes.

Place the disk(s) on the prepared baking sheet, and flatten slightly with a rolling pin.

Prepare the filling: Toss the plums in a bowl with the softened butter and the brown sugar. Spoon the filling onto the center of each disk, and spread it out evenly, leaving $^3/_4$ inch around the edges.

Fold over and pinch the edges to create a rim for the galette. Sprinkle sugar over the top.

Bake for 35 to 40 minutes, until the galettes are dark brown and the plums are bubbling.

Let cool before serving.

nutty apple crisp

We're apple fanatics in our home, buying them in bags at the farmers' market and cooking with them as often as possible. Apples are so easy: they taste great if you bake them on their own, throw them in a pie, or best of all, blanket them in a cozy, nutty, crispy layer of oats. Nothing beats a good warm apple crisp topped with a dollop of organic whipped cream.

FOR THE APPLE FILLING

3 pounds farm−fresh organic Granny Smith or Ida Red apples, cored, peeled, and thinly sliced

1/4 cup firmly packed organic dark−brown sugar

1/2 teaspoon grated organic lemon zest

1 tablespoon organic ground cinnamon

Pinch of freshly grated organic nutmeg

FOR THE CRISP TOPPING

2 sticks (1 cup) organic unsalted butter

1/2 cup chopped organic pecans

1 cup organic rolled oats (not instant or quick−cooking)

1/8 teaspoon organic ground ginger

1/2 teaspoon organic ground cinnamon

1/2 teaspoon salt

3/4 cup firmly packed organic dark−brown sugar or Rapadura (see page 14)

1/2 cup organic whole wheat pastry flour

FOR SERVING

Fresh whipped cream

Preheat the oven to 400°F. Butter a 13 × 9 × 2-inch baking dish or three 6-inch cast-iron skillets and set aside.

In a medium bowl, mix the apples with the brown sugar, lemon zest, cinnamon, and nutmeg. Spread the mixture evenly in the baking dish or skillets.

Using your hands or a fork, mix all the topping ingredients together in a bowl until crumbly.

Sprinkle the topping evenly over the apple mixture, and bake until bubbly and crisp on top, 25 to 30 minutes.

Serve warm, with fresh whipped cream.

there snoring, with the empty cup on the floor beside the bed; about Linda and Pope, Linda and Popé.

He hated Popé more and more. A man can smile and smile and be a villain. Remorseless, treacherous, lecherous, kindless villain. What did the words exactly mean? He only half knew. But their magic was strong and went on rumbling in his head, and somehow it was as though he had never really hated Popé before; never really hated him because he had never been able to say how much he hated him. But now he had these words, these words like drums and singing and magic. These words and the strange story out of which they were taken (he couldn't make head or tail of it, but it was wonderful, wonderful all the same)—they gave him a reason for hating Popé; and they made his hatred more real; they even made Popé himself more real.

One day, when he came in from playing, the door of the inner room was open, and he saw them lying together asleep—white Linda and Popé almost arm under her shoulders and breast, like a black snake and a cup were standing. was snoring.

ared and left a hole. nd rather sick, and steady himself. Re- Like drums, like gic, the words re- head. From being urnt with the rush before his eyes. He him, I'll kill him," ere more words.

in his rage e of his bed the magic explained and in the outer room. "When knife for the meat was lying ce. He picked it up and tiptoed en he is drunk asleep, drunk

and the men of the pueblo hat c res, the seed of the sun seed of the sky—Awona e Fog of Increase. Now he he laid the seeds in the lowest d gradually the seeds began to

calculated later that it must have been welfth birthday) he came home and found ook th e had never seen before lying on the floor in e bedroom. It was a thick book and looked very old. The binding had been eaten by mice; some of its pages were loose and crumpled. He picked it up, looked at the title-page; the book was called *The Complete Works of William Shakespeare.*

Linda was lying on the bed, sipping that horrible stinking mescal out of a cup. "Popé brought it," she said. Her voice was thick and hoarse like somebody else's voice. "It was lying in one of the chests of the Antelope Kiva. It's supposed to have been there for hundreds of years. I expect it's true, because I looked at it, and it seemed to be full of nonsense. Uncivilized. Still, it'll be good enough for you to practise your reading on." She took a last sip, set the cup down on the floor beside the bed, turned over on her side, hiccoughed once or twice and went to sl

He opened the book at random.

> Nay, but to live
> In the rank sweat of an enseamed bed,
> Stew'd in corruption, honeying and mak
> Over the nasty sty . . .

The strange words rolled through his
like talking thunder; like the drums at the
if the drums could have spoken; like the
Corn Song, beautiful, beautiful, so that you
Mitsima saying magic over his feathers a
d his bits of bone and stone—kiathla, tsithl—but

spring and summer

sour cherry–almond tart

| MAKES ONE 10–INCH TART |

Of all the fruits in the world, sour cherries are my favorite. I love their tartness, firm flesh, and dark wine–colored juice. The first stone fruit of the season, they always remind me that summer finally has arrived. I love baking this tart and then eating it all myself.

In the French cookbooks that were handed down from my parents, I've read that the kernels of apricots and other stone fruits have an essence of almond in them, although you'd have to crack the pits and boil and extract the seeds to get at it. I don't bother going to all that trouble; I just use almonds to harmonize with the cherry flavor, and the result is a gorgeous balance of sweet, tart, juicy, and crunchy.

1 pound farm–fresh organic sour cherries,
   pits removed
$3/4$ cup organic cane sugar
2 teaspoons organic almond extract
1 teaspoon grated organic lemon zest
$1/2$ cup organic whole wheat pastry flour
1 cup ground almonds (see Note)

$3/4$ cup firmly packed organic dark–brown
   sugar
1 stick ($1/2$ cup) organic unsalted butter,
   chilled and cut into cubes
1 organic egg yolk
Organic vanilla ice cream or Vanilla Whipped
   Cream (page 180)

Preheat the oven to 400°F and place the oven rack on the lowest level.

In a medium bowl, combine the cherries, cane sugar, almond extract, and lemon zest. Set aside.

In a food processor, combine the flour, ground almonds, and brown sugar. Pulse on and off until the mixture resembles a coarse meal.

Add the butter and egg yolk and pulse on and off for 20 seconds, until the dough gathers into a ball.

Reserving $1/2$ cup of the dough, press the rest onto the bottom and sides of a 10-inch tart pan with a removable bottom.

Spread the cherry mixture on top of the crust, as evenly as possible. Sprinkle the reserved dough over the cherries.

Bake the tart for 55 minutes, or until the crust is lightly browned and the cherry juices are bubbling. (If the sides of the tart start to darken before the baking is done, cover the edges with long pieces of foil so they won't burn.)

Let the tart cool for 10 minutes. Then remove the sides of the pan and transfer the tart to a flat plate. Serve warm or at room temperature, with vanilla ice cream or Vanilla Whipped Cream.

Note: Throw blanched almonds into a food processor or a cleaned-out coffee grinder and grind until as fine as possible, being careful not to overgrind them, creating nut butter.

blake latimer's blueberry pie

| MAKES ONE 9-INCH PIE |

My close friend Quinn Latimer, fellow Californian and poet, shared this pie recipe from her late mother, Blake Latimer. I had the fortune to meet her mother and taste her home-made pies on a few of her Brooklyn visits. Here, the simplicity of the local fruit mixed with the delicate, buttery crust makes true pie perfection.

Quinn wrote this lovely tribute: "To my mother, pies were as necessary as books. After writing and reading into the night, she could often be found in the kitchen, rolling out a pie crust in between chapters of an early Doris Lessing novel, or while taking a break from the Tarkovsky film festival she was conducting in the living room. Somewhere in our fridge there was always a bowl of berries—invariably blueberries or strawberries, sometimes raspberries—melting into the sugar and lemon juice she had thrown in with them. She'd cover the bowl with some plastic wrap, fall asleep with a book on her chest, and wake up in the middle of the night to roll out the pie. In the morning my brother and I would come down the stairs, and there, in the middle of the kitchen table, would be the familiar sight of a golden-brown pie with a lattice top. Sometimes she would cut a word or two from the dough scraps and add it to the top of the pie—our names, or something opaque and philo-sophical like TRUTH—*and it would gleam above the darkened berries below.*

FOR THE ALL—BUTTER PIE CRUST

2 cups organic all—purpose
  flour
1/2 teaspoon salt

14 tablespoons organic unsalted butter,
  chilled and cut into 1/2—inch pieces (see
  Note)
Ice water

FOR THE BLUEBERRY FILLING

2 pints (4 cups) farm—fresh organic
  blueberries
3/4 cup organic cane sugar
1 tablespoon organic arrowroot

2 tablespoons fresh organic lemon
  juice
1 teaspoon grated organic lemon zest
1 teaspoon organic vanilla extract

TO FINISH

1 organic egg

FOR SERVING

Fresh whipped cream

Prepare the pie crust: In a food processor, briefly pulse the flour and salt together. Add the butter and pulse on and off for about 5 seconds, until the mixture forms small pieces. Remove the mixture from the food processor and place it in a bowl.

Add 4 to 6 tablespoons ice water, 1 spoonful at a time, and very briefly knead the dough until it is moist enough to hold together. Form the dough into a ball, wrap it in plastic wrap, and flatten it into a disk. Refrigerate for at least 1 hour.

While dough is chilling, prepare the filling: Combine all the filling ingredients in a medium bowl. Cover the bowl with plastic wrap and refrigerate to let the arrowroot thicken, at least 30 minutes.

Position a rack in the lowest third of the oven and preheat the oven to 400°F.

Divide the dough in half and roll out one half on a lightly floured surface to make a 12^1/$_2$-inch round. Transfer the dough to a 9-inch glass pie dish. Trim the overhang to ^{3}/$_4$ inch.

Spoon the filling into the crust.

Roll out the other dough half on a lightly floured surface to form a 12-inch round. Using a dull knife, cut the dough into roughly ^{1}/$_2$-inch-wide strips. Arrange half the dough strips across the top of the filling. Form a lattice by weaving more dough strips across the first layer of strips, over and under, over and under.

Trim the dough strips even with the overhang on the bottom crust. Tuck the ends of the dough strips and the overhang under, pressing to seal. Crimp the edges with the back of a fork. If you like, use your fingers to pinch the dough scraps into words, such as LOVE, TRUTH, or PEACE, or make a heart shape, and place on the center of the pie.

Beat the egg with 1 tablespoon water. Use a pastry brush to coat the crust with the egg mixture.

Place the pie dish on a baking sheet and bake for 40 to 45 minutes, or until the filling bubbles thickly in the center and the crust is a honey brown.

Let the pie cool, and serve with fresh whipped cream.

Note: For an even more buttery and tender dough, try a high-fat, European-style butter such as Organic Valley's Pasture Butter, which has an 84% butterfat content (higher than the typical organic butter's 80%).

minty strawberry shortcakes

When my husband and I started dating in our early twenties, we traded off making Valentine's Day dinners for each other. Sometimes the themes got elaborate, like the memorable Lady and the Tramp *year, when I crumpled newspaper on the floor, lit red heart-shaped lamps, and cooked heart-shaped meatballs with spaghetti. Eventually, as life became busier, we opted for quiet, simple dinners at our favorite local restaurant. We reinstated the yearly ritual of cooking at home when Clyde was born, but were so bleary with new parenthood that we held our Valentine's Day dinner a few months late, when strawberries were out in full force. My husband whipped up these strawberry shortcakes for dessert, cutting out each one by hand with small heart-shaped cookie cutters. It made my heart swoon: for someone who doesn't bake often, he really made them with love. In this version, I've added the mint to the strawberry for extra summer freshness.*

FOR THE SHORTCAKES

2 cups organic whole wheat pastry flour

1/4 cup organic cane sugar

2 tablespoons baking powder

1/2 teaspoon salt

1 1/2 sticks (3/4 cup) organic unsalted butter, chilled and cut into small cubes

1/2 cup organic buttermilk

1/2 cup organic heavy cream, plus more for brushing

2 teaspoons grated organic lemon zest

Organic raw sugar, for sprinkling

FOR THE STRAWBERRIES

3 pints farm—fresh organic strawberries, hulled and quartered

2 tablespoons thinly sliced fresh organic mint

1/4 cup organic cane sugar

1 teaspoon fresh organic lemon juice (use the lemon you zested for the shortcakes)

FOR THE VANILLA WHIPPED CREAM

1 pint organic heavy cream	Pinch of salt
1/3 cup organic powdered sugar, sifted	1 tablespoon organic vanilla extract

In a food processor, pulse the flour, sugar, baking powder, and salt to combine.

Add the butter, a few cubes at a time, pulsing on and off until the mixture looks like a coarse meal. This should take 20 to 40 seconds. Dump this mixture into a large bowl and set it aside.

In a medium bowl, whisk together the buttermilk, cream, and lemon zest. Add the liquid mixture to the dry mixture, stirring with a fork just until a dough forms.

Lightly flour a work surface. Gently knead the dough on the floured surface a few times, until all the ingredients are combined. Form it into a disk. Place the disk on a baking sheet lined with parchment paper. Lightly sprinkle the disk with flour, and use a rolling pin to flatten the dough to 3/4-inch thickness. Let the dough chill in the refrigerator for 20 minutes.

Meanwhile, preheat the oven to 400°F.

Remove the dough from the refrigerator. Using 2-inch heart-shaped cookie cutters, cut out the shortcakes as close together as possible, so that you're using almost all the dough. Place the heart shapes at least 1 1/2 inches apart on a baking sheet. Brush with cream and sprinkle with raw sugar for sparkle. Reroll the scraps, following the directions until all the dough is used up.

Bake the shortcakes until they are pale brown, 15 to 18 minutes. Remove from the oven and use a spatula to place them on a wire cooling rack.

While the shortcakes are cooling, combine all the strawberry ingredients in a large mixing bowl. Let stand for about 30 minutes, until the strawberry juices come out. (You may need to drain the mixture before placing it on the shortcakes.)

When you are ready to assemble the shortcakes, chill the metal bowl for a standing mixer (or if you're using a hand mixer, a stainless-steel bowl) for about 10 minutes in the freezer. Pour the cream into the chilled bowl and beat with the whisk attachment on low speed, gradually increasing to high speed as the cream thickens. Slowly pour in the powdered sugar, and when the cream has thickened, add the pinch of salt and the vanilla. Continue beating until fully whipped.

To assemble, slice the cooled shortcakes in half and arrange them on individual plates. Spoon $1/4$ cup or more of the strawberry-mint mixture onto the shortcake bottoms, and finish with a dollop of Vanilla Whipped Cream. Place the other halves of the shortcakes on top and devour!

freyja's strawberry-rhubarb pie

| MAKES ONE 9–INCH PIE |

I've enjoyed many fantastic meals with my good friend Freyja Gallagher, a fellow foodie whom I met after I moved to Brooklyn. One of her specialties is this pie, and she bakes it frequently when rhubarb and strawberries are in season. (She's lucky enough to live across the street from the farmers' market, so she can run over in her pajamas and grab the first baskets of fruit!) For her pie, she uses tapioca, a more natural and less chalky-tasting thickener than the commonly used cornstarch. She likes to cut small hearts into the top of the pie, to release the steam from the bubbling filling and to give it a home-kissed touch.

FOR THE CRUST

2 cups organic whole wheat pastry flour
2 teaspoons organic cane sugar
1 teaspoon salt

2 sticks (1 cup) organic unsalted butter,
    cut into small pieces, chilled (see Note)
Ice water

FOR THE FILLING

2 cups farm fresh organic strawberries,
    hulled and sliced
About 6 stalks farm–fresh organic
    rhubarb, cut into $1/3$-inch pieces (2 cups)

3 tablespoons quick–cooking tapioca
1 cup organic cane sugar
Grated zest of 1 organic lemon
2 tablespoons organic unsalted butter

TO FINISH

1 organic egg, beaten
2 tablespoons organic whole milk

2 tablespoons organic turbinado sugar
    (large–crystal raw sugar), for sprinkling

FOR SERVING

Crème fraîche or Vanilla Whipped Cream (page 180)

Place 1 cup of the flour, 1 teaspoon of the sugar, and $^1/_2$ teaspoon of the salt in a food processor and pulse to combine.

Cut 1 stick of the butter into 8 pieces, and pulse them with the dry ingredients until well combined. The mixture should have a sandy, grainy texture.

Gradually sprinkle in 2 tablespoons ice water while continuing to pulse. The dough will become cohesive and form a ball.

Remove the dough from the food processor and shape it into a disk about 1 inch high and 4 inches across. Wrap it in plastic wrap and place it in the refrigerator to chill for at least 20 minutes.

Repeat with the remaining half of the crust ingredients.

While the dough is chilling, make the filling: Combine all the filling ingredients except the butter in a large bowl. Mix well and let stand for at least 15 minutes.

Preheat the oven to 450°F.

Roll out the dough on a lightly floured work surface to form 2 rounds of even thickness, about 12 inches in diameter.

Place 1 round in a 9-inch pie pan, pressing it into the bottom and down the sides of the pan. Add the fruit filling to the pie shell and dot with the butter.

Cover the pie with the remaining round. Turn the edges of the bottom crust over the top edges and flute together. To allow steam to vent, make holes in the top crust. You can create a decorative pattern with a fork or a cookie cutter. I like heart cutouts, but simple slits with a knife will do the job too.

In a small bowl, beat the egg and milk together. Brush the top crust with the egg-milk mixture, and sprinkle the turbinado sugar over it for a sparkly effect.

Bake for 10 minutes. Reduce the heat to 350°F and bake for 35 to 40 minutes, or until golden brown.

Let the pie cool on a wire rack for 2 hours. Serve with crème fraîche or Vanilla Whipped Cream.

Note: Make sure the butter is well chilled. You can place cut-up pieces in the freezer for a few minutes right before using so that it is very cold.

colombe's wheat-free lavender apricot crisp

| MAKES EIGHT 4–INCH RAMEKINS |

Lavender isn't just for tea sachets or fragrance; using fresh lavender in your sweets—cookies, ice creams, pies, and crisps—highlights bold fruit flavors. This is a summertime favorite created by my college friend Colombe Jacobsen-Derstine, an amazing chef who focuses on natural and healthful cooking. We always meet in the city to try out new bakeries and discuss the latest sweets trends in New York City. When apricots are in season, this wonderfully aromatic combination of lavender and apricot really hits the spot!

2 pounds ripe organic apricots (16 to 18 apricots), pitted
$3/4$ cup organic cane sugar or maple sugar, plus extra for sprinkling
1 tablespoon plus 1 teaspoon organic arrowroot or cornstarch

$2 1/2$ tablespoons dried organic lavender flowers (found at specialty stores and farmers' markets)
$1 1/2$ cups organic oat flour (see Note)
Pinch of salt
$1/3$ cup organic unsalted butter, melted
$1/3$ cup organic plain yogurt

Position a rack in the center of the oven and preheat the oven to 400°F. Butter eight 4-inch ramekins, and set them aside.

Cut the apricots into 1-inch pieces and place them in a medium bowl.

In a small bowl, whisk together $1/4$ cup of the sugar and the arrowroot. Sprinkle this mixture over the fruit, add the lavender flowers, and toss to combine.

Spoon the fruit into the prepared ramekins, leaving $1/4$ inch at the top for the crisp topping.

Combine the oat flour, remaining $^1/_2$ cup sugar, and the salt in a medium bowl. Stir in the melted butter. Add the yogurt and mix until everything comes together into a dough.

Using the back of a spoon, spread the topping evenly over the apricot mixture so that it is flush with the rim of the ramekin.

Place the ramekins on a baking sheet and bake for 20 to 25 minutes, or until the topping is golden.

Enjoy warm or at room temperature, with a sprinkling of sugar on top.

Note: You can make oat flour at home by simply processing rolled oats in a blender or a food processor until powdery.

children's goodies

THE RECIPES IN THIS CHAPTER are Clyde's favorites—plus a few that I like to make for friends when I'm feeling whimsical. It's important to teach children about food: buying it from local farmers, visiting berry farms in the summer, cooking together. When baking with kids, keep it simple, and be extra-patient so they don't feel overwhelmed. Clyde has had a few "baking incidents," such as when he whisked the dry ingredients right out of the bowl or knocked the softened stick of butter off the counter and onto my foot. It was very moisturizing and made for a good laugh!

Clyde has always been a picky eater, but when he gets involved in making something, he's more likely to try it. Cooking and baking with your kids opens their palates and their minds more than just putting a new food in front of them. Luckily for me, Ruby is mellow and very open to experimenting with food. Because she's younger, I like to make snacks for her that are easy to transport, like her favorite Millet Muffins (page 207), which are made with a bit of honey but are savory and full of whole grains.

Both my kids bring joy to my life, and I find so much inspiration when I look at the world through their perspectives. Clyde wears a mini apron, and we have matching bandanas to cover our hair while cooking. When he couldn't find his "baking bandana" once, he came up with the idea to wear his bicycle helmet! Baking with

Ruby's first birthday

Jackson and Clyde: best friends forever

Ruby

Erin, a "cool" girl

him has brought back so many memories of my own childhood and reminds me how precious that time is, giving you a chance to talk about funny ideas or to hear your children's challenging questions. I get ideas from Clyde's drawings of colorful planets and outer space, the autumn leaves he's glued onto a piece of paper, and his painted toilet-paper dioramas showing the metamorphosis of a butterfly. Clyde is bursting with the excitement and wonder of learning something for the first time, and his enthusiasm is contagious. Most mornings in our house start off with a dance party, and I know we're building fun memories in the kitchen, with all the baking, cooking, and booty shaking that goes on.

When your hairnet is nowhere to be found, a bicycle helmet will do.

clyde's sugar cookies

| MAKES 3 DOZEN COOKIES |

When Clyde bakes, he goes all out: He pulls up a chair, puts on his blue train apron, ties a red bandana on his head, and lays out all his special baking tools to help Mom. We make these cookies all the time and decorate them differently for each occasion.

When all Clyde's small cousins get together during the holidays, I bake these into different shapes and let them have a cookie decorating party.

3 sticks (1 1/2 cups) organic unsalted butter, softened
2 cups organic cane sugar
2 organic eggs
1 tablespoon organic vanilla extract
1/2 teaspoon salt

4 cups organic all—purpose flour, sifted
Candy Glue (page 196)
For sprinkling: colored sugar, dried shredded organic coconut, chopped dried fruit, or chocolate chips

Line 2 baking sheets with parchment paper, and cut 2 more sheets of parchment the same size. Set aside.

In a standing mixer fitted with the paddle attachment, cream the butter and sugar on medium speed until creamy and fluffy, 3 to 5 minutes, scraping down the sides of the bowl with a rubber spatula.

With the mixer on low speed, add the eggs, one at a time, beating until incorporated. Add the vanilla and salt. Then slowly add the sifted flour, beating until combined. Scrape down the sides of the bowl.

Divide the dough in half, and place a mound of dough on each parchment-lined baking sheet. Cover the dough with the other sheets of parchment and use a rolling pin to flatten the dough to about a $\frac{1}{4}$-inch thickness (this method avoids making the dough stiffer by adding extra flour). It's okay if the dough sticks to the paper; once the dough is cold, the paper will peel right off.

Chill the dough for 15 minutes.

Meanwhile, preheat the oven to 350°F.

Sprinkle a small amount of flour on your work surface. Dip cookie cutters into the flour to prevent them from sticking to the dough.

Remove the dough from the refrigerator, peel off the top parchment, and quickly cut out shapes close to one another, pulling away the excess dough as you work. If the dough gets too soft while you are cutting, simply refrigerate it again to make it harder and easier to handle.

Chill the cutout cookies for about 8 minutes.

Remove the cookies from the refrigerator, and bake on the parchment-lined baking sheets for about 13 minutes, or until they're light brown around the bottom edges.

Let the cookies cool for a minute on the baking sheets. Then use a spatula to transfer them to a wire rack and let them cool completely.

When the cookies have cooled, place them on wax paper. Use a small butter knife to spread the Candy Glue (page 196) onto the cookies, and then sprinkle colored sugar, shredded coconut, dried fruit, or chocolate chips onto the glue.

crazy coconut cookie pops

1 batch Clyde's Sugar Cookie dough
Candy Glue (recipe follows)
1/2 cup organic dried currants (for eyes)

1/4 cup organic whole cashews,
    cut in half (for noses)
Lollipop sticks

Preheat the oven to 350°F and roll the chilled dough out to a 1/4-inch thickness.

Use a drinking glass or a round cookie cutter to cut rounds as close to one another as possible. Reroll the scraps of dough and cut out more cookies.

Place the cookies on prepared baking sheets and attach lollipop sticks ¼ to ½ inch from the bottom. The sticks should end in the center of the cookie. Push the dough over any exposed stick.

Bake for 10 to 12 minutes until slightly golden brown.

Once the cookies are cooled, spread candy glue on the top and btom of each cookie, pressing shredded coconut into the glue to ate hair and a beard. Using a toothpick, dab two dots of glue for and press the currants into the dots. Add a single dot for the ca nose. Let the cookie pops air-dry for about 30 minutes before y devour them like a cannibal.

candy glue

| MAKES ABOUT 1/2 CUP |

1 cup organic powdered sugar
1 teaspoon organic vanilla extract

2 tablespoons organic heavy
    cream

Sift the sugar into a bowl. Add the vanilla and cream, and whisk until glue-like. (The Candy Glue should not be stiff; it should be gooey.) Use immediately.

easy "posh" pudding

| MAKES 2 1/2 CUPS (ABOUT 4 SERVINGS) |

Clyde loves learning about different parts of the world. I have tried my hardest to give him examples of what kinds of accents there are. (The concept of an accent is difficult for a four-year-old to grasp!) For some reason, the word "posh" spoken in a horrible fake British accent cracks him up.

I call this "posh" pudding because it can appear fancy and sophisticated but it's also easy for kids to help make—and they love to eat it. It's adapted from a recipe given to me almost ten years ago by Susan Moseman, mother of my friend Freyja Gallagher. For grown-ups, I serve it in antique teacups, spoon on some fresh whipped cream, and sprinkle candied hazelnuts on top; and to serve kids, I use footed ice cream bowls, which makes them feel as if they're having a big-kid treat!

1/4 cup organic cornstarch
1/2 cup organic unsweetened cocoa powder
1/2 cup organic cane sugar

2 cups organic whole milk, chilled
2 teaspoons organic vanilla extract
Candied Hazelnuts (optional; recipe follows)

Combine the cornstarch, cocoa, and sugar in a small heavy-bottomed saucepan.

With the pan on low heat, slowly pour in the cold milk, whisking to combine.

Increase the heat to medium-high and continue whisking (to prevent any lumps) until the mixture boils, about 1 minute. Remove the pan from the heat and stir in the vanilla.

Let cool in the refrigerator with plastic wrap on the surface to prevent a skin from forming. Serve in individual cups, ramekins, or glasses. Garnish with candied hazelnuts, if desired.

The perfect party treat

Mexican-Chocolate Pudding

Add ¹/₂ teaspoon ground organic cinnamon and a pinch of cayenne pepper to the dry ingredients. Top the pudding with a dollop of whipped cream and a sprinkling of black sea salt.

candied hazelnuts

¹/₂ cup firmly packed organic dark—brown sugar

1 cup chopped organic hazelnuts

Lay a piece of aluminum foil on your work surface.

Melt the brown sugar in a saucepan over low heat. Add the nuts and bring the mixture to a boil without stirring. When the sugar starts to deepen in color and a candy thermometer reads 236°F, pour the mixture onto the foil and let it cool completely.

Break the hardened hazelnut brittle into pieces and sprinkle them on top of puddings, cakes, or cupcakes, for a little added crunch.

Note: You can substitute cashews, almonds, pecans, or any other of your favorite nuts.

no-bake honey-peanut dough creatures

| MAKES 2 CUPS DOUGH |

Clyde and I make this dough on rainy days, or whenever he needs a little quality time with Mom. We add additional nuts and other goodies (see suggestions) to make it more nutritious and to create kooky creatures and animals. There's no limit to children's imaginations and to what they might sculpt with this dough. And the best part is that they can eat the heads off their nutritious snack!

1 $1/2$ cups natural peanut butter
$1/2$ cup organic honey
1 teaspoon organic ground cinnamon

1 cup organic toasted wheat germ
$1/2$ cup organic ground flaxseed

ADDITIONS (OPTIONAL)
$1/4$ cup shredded organic unsweetened
   coconut
$1/4$ cup organic sesame seeds
$1/4$ cup organic sunflower seeds
For eyes and noses:
   organic cashews
   organic raisins
   organic chocolate chips
   organic dried cranberries

For arms and legs:
   organic pretzel sticks
   organic carrots
   organic dried pineapple
   organic celery
   organic almonds

In a medium bowl, combine the peanut butter and honey.

Mix in the cinnamon wheat germ, flaxseed, and any additions.

Knead, sculpt, and play with the dough, using add-ins to make faces, animals, people, monsters, and other kooky creations.

Store the dough in an airtight container (or else it will develop a crust on the outside). This will keep in the refrigerator for 2 to 3 days.

chocolate plastic dough

This is an adaptation of a chocolate plastique recipe I learned in one of my master cake-decorating classes. With an elastic texture and a taste similar to that of Tootsie Rolls, the dough rolls out thin, so it's easy to cut out shapes with cookie cutters or to make animals, robots, or any other figures, such as flowers and balls. Although the dough is easy to make, it will require a little muscle strength to knead it at first.

    I like to use a small handful at a time, rolling small balls and flattening them for polka dots, or rolling long "snakes" with Clyde to make animals. You can use the same edible additions listed in the recipe for the No-Bake Honey-Peanut Dough Creatures (page 200).

12 ounces organic bittersweet chocolate, chopped into pieces (see Note)

¹⁄₂ cup organic light corn syrup

Melt the chocolate in a small heavy-bottomed saucepan over low heat. As soon as it has melted, remove the pan from the heat and add the corn syrup. The mixture will begin to thicken.

Using a rubber spatula, scrape the mixture onto a large piece of plastic wrap.

Flatten the dough to a ¹⁄₂-inch thickness, cover it completely in plastic wrap, and chill it in the refrigerator until completely hardened, about 24 hours.

Let the dough sit on the counter for 30 minutes to warm to room temperature. Then, using all your strength, break the dough into pieces and soften it by kneading and squeezing. Although it may seem very hard (or impossible), the dough will become smooth and pliable after a good 4 to 5 minutes of kneading!

Use a lightly floured rolling surface and pin to smooth out the dough, or use your hands to shape the dough as you would with clay. The dough will harden when refrigerated and last for 3 to 4 days covered in plastic wrap or in a plastic container. If you overhandle the dough, it will get sticky, so be sure to let it cool if it starts to get too soft.

Note: I tried this once with a bag of semisweet chocolate chips. The plastic seemed the same, but when it came time to knead it, the cocoa butter in the chips seemed to make it a little gooey, although it was still workable.

A nice, meaty chocolate salami is
the best chic gag gift.

chocolate salami

When I traveled to Italy as a shoe designer, I visited all the markets and grocery stores after long days visiting factories. I sought out food that seemed unusual or hard to find in New York at the time, like raw cheeses and hand-bottled olive oil. On one such trip I found a shop that sold faux "salami" that looked exactly like meat, made out of chocolate and crushed wafers and wrapped in a white casing.

I was quite the smuggler, flying home with my unpasteurized cheese hidden inside rolls of socks and the chocolate salami stowed in my carry-on. I made it through Customs somehow, even though I smelled like rotten feet because of the cheese. When I got home, my boyfriend (now my husband) and I enjoyed the most amazing meal from my contraband loot. Inspired by that funny fake salami, I made a bunch for holiday presents one year.

For a fun twist, you can create strings of mini wieners like the ones you see hanging in cartoon butcher-shop windows. Simply sculpt small "wieners" instead of a large "salami" and attach kitchen twine around the edges, connecting three "wieners" end to end. Wrap them up in parchment paper to simulate butcher's wax paper and present them in a box as a silly—and delicious—gift.

1 pound organic wafer cookies (I like the hazelnut—filled wafers, and Clyde likes the vanilla kind. You can also use graham crackers.)

12 ounces organic semisweet or milk—chocolate chips (milk chocolate makes the salami color lighter, and the salami sweeter)

$1/2$ stick ($1/4$ cup) organic unsalted butter

$1/4$ cup organic sweetened condensed milk (available at Trader Joe's and other stores)

$1/2$ cup organic almonds, toasted and chopped

Powdered sugar, for rolling

Place the wafers in a sealable plastic bag, seal the bag, and crush them with a mallet or a kid's wooden hammer until some small chunks remain but most of cookies are crumbled. (Clyde loves to do this part!) Set aside.

In the top of a double boiler set over simmering water, or with short bursts in a microwave, melt the chocolate chips and butter together until the chocolate is just melted. Remove from the heat, stir to combine, and set aside to cool.

Stir the condensed milk into the cooled chocolate mixture. Mix in the crushed wafers and $1/4$ cup of the toasted almonds (to resemble chunks of salami fat), stirring until the dough is stiff. Use your hands to finish the mixing.

Shape the dough into a salami-shaped log. Press the remaining $1/4$ cup almonds onto the outside. Pinch the ends to resemble a salami. Wrap the salami in aluminum foil and refrigerate it for at least 1 hour.

Sprinkle powdered sugar on a work surface. Roll the log back and forth in the sugar, coating the entire salami.

Using a serrated knife, slice the salami. Serve it on a wooden cutting board for an especially authentic look!

ruby's millet muffins

| MAKES ABOUT 25 MINI MUFFINS OR 14 STANDARD MUFFINS |

Before Ruby turned one, I experimented with baking something for her that contained only whole grains and that was portable, like a bread or a muffin—and something my husband would like to eat too! I came up with this crumbly, hearty, slightly sweet muffin brimming with fruit and crunchy millet—totally delicious! At Ruby's first birthday party, I served these for her baby friends, but then all my adult friends ended up eating them too. Now they are my go-to recipe when I want to bake something healthy that everyone can enjoy.

2 1/4 cups organic whole wheat flour

3/4 cup organic millet

1 teaspoon baking powder

1 teaspoon baking soda

1/4 teaspoon salt

1/4 cup whole organic flaxseed

1/4 teaspoon ground organic cinnamon

1 cup organic buttermilk

1 organic egg

1/4 cup organic vegetable oil

1/4 cup organic unsweetened applesauce

1/2 cup organic honey

1 teaspoon organic vanilla extract

1 cup organic blueberries, preferably farm—fresh

Preheat the oven to 400°F. Line mini or conventional muffin pans with cupcake liners and set aside. If you are making mini muffins for little ones, it is easier to spray the pan with nonstick spray so you don't have to peel the liner away.

In a large bowl, mix the flour, millet, baking powder, baking soda, salt, flaxseed, and cinnamon.

In a separate bowl, mix the buttermilk, egg, vegetable oil, apple-sauce, honey, and vanilla.

Stir the buttermilk mixture into the flour mixture just until evenly moist. Fold in the blueberries, and transfer the batter to the prepared muffin cups.

Bake conventional muffins for 15 minutes and mini muffins for 12 to 13 minutes, or until a toothpick inserted in the center of a muffin comes out clean.

Remove the muffins from the pans and let cool on a wire rack.

sweet-potato cookies

| MAKES 2 DOZEN COOKIES |

I've adapted these easy and wholesome cookies from one of my favorite health–oriented cookbooks, Nourishing Traditions *by Sally Fallon. A fantastic treat for kids, they're sweetened naturally with sweet potatoes and maple syrup and contain no refined sugar. I make these for Clyde's snack day or class parties at school, and because they bake to a gorgeous orange color, they're also perfect at any fall or Thanksgiving table.*

1 cup cooked, peeled, and cubed organic
   farm–fresh sweet potato or winter
   squash (such as butternut)
1 stick ($^1/2$ cup) organic unsalted butter,
   softened
$^3/4$ cup organic maple syrup
1 organic egg
$^1/2$ teaspoon sea salt

$^1/2$ teaspoon ground organic nutmeg
1 teaspoon ground organic cinnamon
1 teaspoon baking soda
2 cups organic whole wheat flour
$^1/2$ cup chopped organic raisins
   (optional)
$^1/2$ cup organic pecans, toasted
$^1/4$ cup raw sugar, for garnish (optional)

Preheat the oven to 325°F. Cover 2 baking sheets with aluminum foil, and butter the foil. Set aside.

Combine the sweet potato or squash, butter, maple syrup, and egg in a food processor, and pulse until smooth, about 1 minute.

Add the salt, nutmeg, cinnamon, baking soda, and flour, and pul in 10-second bursts until mixed.

Transfer the dough to a bowl, and stir in the raisins if using.

Form the dough into walnut-size balls and place them about 2 inches apart on the prepared baking sheets. Using a fork, flatte each cookie. Press $^1/2$ teaspoon of the pecans on top of each one.

Bake for about 20 minutes, or until the edges darken.

Let the cookies cool completely on the baking sheets before removing them with a spatula. Sprinkle some raw sugar on top of the cookies for a sparkly effect.

Store the cookies in an airtight container in the refrigerator for up to 1 week.

design
techniques

WHEN IT COMES TO FABULOUS parties, weddings, or other special events, preparing a beautiful cake requires planning and loads of patience. Many times I've envisioned something spectacular, and either my vision has fallen short or the cake has turned out even better than what I had in mind. Baking and decorating take time and shouldn't be rushed. That said, life brims with activity and unexpected surprises, so try your best and laugh at any mishaps.

When designing a cake, it's best to start planning at least a week ahead of time so that you can make sure you have all the ingredients on hand and have considered the decorations. If you're making sugar-paste flowers, you'll need at least a day to sculpt them and give them time to dry. If you need to buy food coloring, give yourself enough time to order it online or to stop by your cake-supply store.

I start all my cake ideas off with a sketch, a photocopy of an old picture, or a tear sheet from a magazine. Inspiration for cakes can come from anywhere and anything. I see it in stylish women on the subway, foreign fashion and interior magazines, old masters paintings in museums—even when I'm at the park with my kids, looking at the skyline.

I keep a small notebook with me at all times to jot down ideas as they happen.

COLORING AND DECORATION
SECRETS TO MASTERING SOPHISTICATED LOOKS

I'm constantly on the lookout for new ideas to decorate my cakes and sweets. Sometimes it's a matter of browsing through fashion magazines and applying seasonal trends such as metallics or bright colors to a cake. I flip through old Betty Crocker cookbooks for ideas that I can adapt in a more sophisticated way. I always look for vintage cookbooks, flower and gardening books, and old home decor books when I'm at thrift stores or on eBay.

COLORS

For a recent a birthday party, I tinted Vanilla Whipped Buttercream (page 84) a pale yellow. After the party, the host called me to ask me about the yellow frosting. "It was so amazing; what was it?" Little did she know that she had tasted it numerous times when it wasn't tinted a color. It's true after all: People eat with their eyes, and simply tinting frosting can affect their taste buds.

As I've mentioned, I use commercial-grade food coloring when tinting my frostings and fillings. I've experimented with many types of natural food coloring (such as beet) and unfortunately, the results were always wimpy and pale. Although the food coloring I use isn't certified organic, I feel comfortable using it since a tiny amount goes a long way.

I love to use colors in unique ways. Cakes shouldn't always be subject to pretty pastels or expected colors. As a guideline, I prepare a bright frosting to *fill* my cakes, especially when the cake is frosted with Melted Chocolate Ganache (page 140) or Shiny Mocha Glaze (page 64)—it's a hidden surprise after people finish drooling over your stellar decorations. There's something chic and whimsical about slicing into a gorgeous, decadent cake to find hot-pink frosting inside. Also, serving the unexpected color makes the statement that you're serious about beauty, and about making something fabulous.

My favorite color combinations

- Salmon—colored flowers with gray piped centers, yellow frosting inside
- Lime—green flowers with gold centers, hot—pink frosting inside
- Lemon—yellow flowers with hot—pink centers, baby—blue frosting inside
- Chocolate flowers with acid—yellow stamens, gray frosting (I do this a lot for men's birthdays and groom cakes)
- Yellow or white flowers on Wedgwood—blue frosting (something about my mother's Wedgwood bowls keeps inspiring me, and I can't shake it!); filled with salmon pink frosting
- A stark and unexpected accent, like black flowers, with any pastel—color frosting, like peach, lavender, or mint green.

Black daisies make a chic contrast.

DECORATIONS

When I decorate a cake, I mix and match the cake flavor, inside filling, and outer icing with whatever theme I have in mind for the dessert. For example, when I designed a cake for the Audubon Society in Brooklyn, I knew I wanted a Wedgwood-blue frosting, so I ruled out the chocolate ganache. For bright frostings, I use either a sweet buttercream or a whipped buttercream for easy tinting. For a more sophisticated look, I lean toward the chocolate ganache frosting. The presentation is more dramatic with bright flowers or shimmery accents.

Your cake size will determine your ingredients and will help you estimate the amount of decorations to make. For example, if I'm planning on a three-tiered cake, I need to have a good range of flower sizes on hand. An eight-inch cake will require more large flowers and probably fewer small flowers. If the cake is for a more casual family gathering, I may decide to prepare another kind of decoration, such as candied lime or lemon slices (see page 74) or to pipe oversized circles on a cake.

I prefer decorations that I can make in quantity and store for future use. That allows me to add a touch of chic to a last-minute dessert. It's easiest to think of decorating in categories:

1. SCULPTED SUGAR: which requires time to sculpt and dry

2. PIPED DECORATIONS: elegant and easy touches

3. CHOCOLATE DECORATIONS: which can be made while your cake or sweets cool on the wire rack

4. METALLIC POWDER DUSTING: dazzling finishes for cakes and cupcakes

Frosting a Cake

- For small cakes, spread the frosting on top first, then on the sides, generously load—
  ing your cake with frosting.
- For larger cakes, always do a crumb coating—a thin coat of icing that traps any loose
  crumbs so that they are not visible in the frosting. Spread a thin layer of frosting on
  the cake first; then chill it; and then frost it again for a crumb—free frosting. For
  softened edges, hold the spatula at a 45—degree angle and apply slight pressure as
  you move the spatula across the top.

Sugar Sculpting: Making Flowers, Leaves, and Other Decorations

Modern sugar flowers are a simple and chic decoration that I use frequently, for all kinds of cakes.

CUTTERS

When I first started making sugar-paste flowers, I simply went to my local cake-supply shop and bought a few sizes of dogwood cutters, which are the flower shapes I use on my popular chocolate Love Blossom cakes (page 31).

Gumpaste cutters are typically smaller than standard cookie cutters and will allow you to be more detailed when making flowers for a cake. I've used cookie cutters for some cakes, but since they are larger, I limit them to specific kids' cakes or to more geometric

A smattering of sugar-paste flowers

gumpaste cutters

shapes. You can order gumpaste cutters online, or find them
in craft stores as well as some housewares shops. I love www.sugar-
craft.com for its vast selection of cutters, categorized by theme.

When sculpting sugar-paste flowers, using various sizes on a cake
will give it sophistication and dimension. Small flowers fit perfectly
in the crook of a two-tier cake and create a sense of movement
between the larger flowers. Buy cutters in a few sizes, so that you
have a range to work with. You can layer the smaller flowers inside
the larger sizes, or come up with patterns of alternating small and
large flowers around the rim of the cake. The combinations are
endless.

I still prefer to use my old dogwood cutters to create basic flower
shapes because they're clean and modern. You can jazz them up with
dotted piping in the center or stack them in alternating directions to
create depth. If you're starting your cutter collection, buy these first.
The other flower shapes I use most often are jasmine and rose calyx

cutters. Traditionally, bakers use these for sculpting traditional, realistic flowers, but I find they also make beautiful miniature flowers. When shopping for cutters, consider their shape and envision how they'll look in a bright color on a cake (rather than what the label on the box says). I've used rose-petal cutters to make leaves, for example. I also keep on hand a bunch of small cookie cutters shaped in scalloped circles or ovals for a nice variety of shapes.

MAKING SUGAR PASTE

Sugar paste, or gumpaste, is a sugar-based dough used for ornamental purposes. It has the texture and elasticity of Play-Doh, and can be rolled thin for making flowers or any other types of sculpted decoration. It dries very hard, and if stored properly, will keep indefinitely. It's perfect for making realistic flowers, bows, and endless other decorations and can be tinted in bright colors. It tastes sort of like sugary cardboard.

I usually make a large batch of homemade sugar paste; the following recipe yields almost 2 pounds, which lasts a while. Many of the ingredients that create the elastic yet doughy texture are derivatives of guar gum, a plant product that is used in foods such as chewing gum. It's not yet available in an organic form; however, if you use organic sugar, organic corn syrup, and organic vegetable shortening, you'll have more control over the quality of your ingredients. If the recipe seems too complicated, premade gumpaste is available at most cake-supply shops, making it easy for you to experiment. I buy it if I run out or if a big order comes up and I haven't made enough of my own.

homemade sugar paste

| MAKES 2 POUNDS |

This is a recipe for gumpaste that I adapted from the recipe Toba Garrett uses at the Institute of Culinary Education in Manhattan. Toba has been a professional cake decorator for over twenty years and probably can make a bouquet of realistic flowers in her sleep! The original recipe also can be found in her book The Well-Decorated Cake. *This recipe yields a large amount of paste, so wrap whatever you don't use well in plastic wrap, place it in a freezer bag, and refrigerate it for up to a month.*

1 tablespoon (1 envelope) organic gelatin
$1/2$ cup organic light corn syrup
2 tablespoons glycerin (available at cake-supply stores)

2 pounds organic powdered sugar, plus more as needed
1 teaspoon Spectrum organic shortening
2 teaspoons tylose (available online and at cake-supply stores)

Pour $1/4$ cup cold water into a stainless-steel bowl, sprinkle the gelatin on top of the water, and let it soften for a few minutes.

Place the bowl on top of a saucepan partially filled with simmering water, and let it warm for a few minutes, until the gelatin dissolves.

Add the corn syrup and glycerin, whisking until the mixture is smooth. Remove the bowl from the heat.

Sift the powdered sugar in another stainless-steel bowl. Make a well in the center of the powdered sugar, and pour the warm gelatin mixture into the center. Use a rubber spatula to mix, and once incorporated, use your hands to knead the gumpaste into a dough.

Continue kneading the dough, adding more powdered sugar as necessary to form a firm mass. Rub $^1/_2$ teaspoon of the shortening in your hands and knead it into the dough.

Shape the dough into a disk and pour the tylose onto the center. Rub the remaining $^1/_2$ teaspoon shortening in your hands and knead the paste for 3 to 5 minutes until thoroughly combined.

Double-wrap the dough in plastic wrap and let it rest in the refrigerator for at least 24 hours.

Remove the dough from the refrigerator and let it come to room temperature. Pinch off a handful of dough to work with at a time. You may want to rub a small bit of vegetable shortening in your hands if the dough is too sticky. Make sure you keep the reserved dough well wrapped in plastic wrap, then place in a zippered freezer bag, to prevent it from drying out.

COLORING SUGAR PASTE

Your work surface should be smooth and nonporous, such as glass, stainless steel, or even a marble board, which you can buy at most housewares shops. Warm the sugar paste in your hand. It will probably be stiff in the beginning. It needs to become a little elastic, but not too sticky (sort of the way Play-Doh feels in your hand). If the paste starts sticking to your hands, add some cornstarch to stiffen it up. Note that the more cornstarch you add, the quicker your paste will dry.

Dip a toothpick in a small amount of food coloring. Insert the toothpick inside the ball of sugar paste. As you remove the toothpick, close the sugar paste around the food coloring. Knead, pull, and mash the dough to evenly distribute the color.

CUTTING SUGAR—PASTE SHAPES

Spread a small amount of cornstarch on your work surface and on top of the dough. Using a plastic roller, roll the dough until it is thin, 1/16 to 1/8 inch.

Sprinkle a mound of cornstarch to the side. Each time you cut into the dough, dip your cutters in the cornstarch so that they won't stick. Cut the shapes out as close to one another as possible, and then gather up the scraps and reroll them.

After cutting out the shapes, transfer them to a foam pad for sculpting. (Foam pads are sold at specialty cake-supply shops and are used specifically for molding and sculpting gumpaste shapes.)

Sculpting tools, foam pad, plastic roller, and a sprinkle of cornstarch

SCULPTING SUGAR PASTE

For sculpting you'll need a ball and neck tool to give your creations dimension and volume.

To make love blossoms   Starting with one petal at a time, gently rub a light amount of cornstarch on the surface (not so much that it is visible, but just enough so that the ball tool doesn't stick to the flower). Applying slight pressure, move the ball in a circular motion to create depth in the petal. The edges of the petal will curl up slightly, but be careful not to apply too much pressure or you'll rip the petal. If you like, you can also roll the ball over the edge of each petal as you go along. This will eliminate the sharp edges left by the cutters.

Use the ball tool to create dimension in each petal.

Love Blossom
flowers

To make a bird's nest and eggs Wrap a round-bottomed glass or cup in a layer of plastic wrap. Tint I cup sugar paste dark brown, and roll out thin ropes of varying lengths. Starting at the top of the cup, lay out the longer pieces so that they overlap and cross one another. Gently press the strips to secure them. Keep pressing additional pieces on top, and work your way down the sides to create a nest. Let the nest dry for at least I day. Then gently pull the nest off the cup.

To make the eggs, tint I/4 cup gumpaste a desired color and roll it into egg shapes, with one end slightly tapered. Fill a small bowl with either lemon juice or a clear alcohol such as vodka, and add a pinch of metallic gold dust. Dip the brush in the mixture. Pull the bristles of the brush back and then release them, so that the metallic liquid splatters the egg. Let the eggs dry. Place in the bird's nest.

MAKING THE NEST

MAKING THE EGGS

To make daisies   When I make daisies, sometimes I roll the dough a bit thicker than usual, around 1/4 inch, because the petals are less likely to become fragile and break off. There is a multitude of petals here; don't forget to dip the cutter in cornstarch each time you cut. Once the petals are cut, use the large ball tip to apply slight pressure from the center of the petal moving outward to create some slight dimension inside.

Bees   It's easy to make bees for Uncle Gravy's Apple Cake (page 53). Color a small batch of sugar paste with lemon-yellow coloring. Pinch off a pea-size amount of paste and roll it into a ball. Using your middle finger and thumb, roll the ball gently back and forth until it takes on an elongated oval shape. Let it dry on a paper towel. Once it is dry, paint stripes on the shape, using a small paintbrush with dark-brown or black luster dust diluted with lemon juice. Cut parchment paper into a 1-inch strip and fold it in half. Cut out an oval shape while the paper is folded, so that when it opens it resembles rounded wings. Some online baking-supply sources carry edible rice paper, which looks and acts just like parchment paper and makes your bees edible! Place a dot of water on the fold line and attach the painted bee to the center. Let dry.

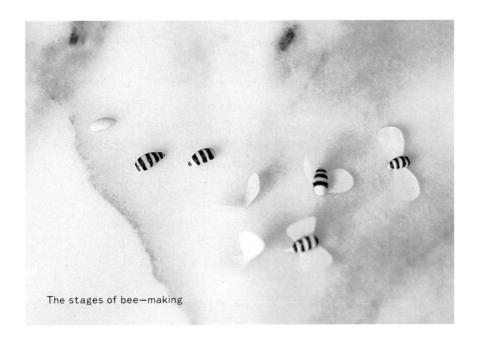

The stages of bee—making

Butterflies   Tint the sugar paste a pale color, such as lilac, pink, yellow, aqua, green, gray, or white. (With light colors you can hand-paint the butterflies and the designs will show beautifully.) Before you roll out the dough, prepare the drying setup for the butterflies: Turn over a recycled egg carton and cut a piece of aluminum foil or parchment paper 2 1/2 inches wide and long enough to fit down the center of the carton. Fold the foil or paper in half, and place it between the rows of ridges in the carton. This setup will allow the wings to dry at the correct angle.

Follow the rolling instructions for the sugar paste, and cut out the shapes with a butterfly cutter.

Use the ball tools to add dimension to the wings, or for a more modern butterfly, leave the thickness as is. You can also use a butterfly cookie cutter. Simply fold the cutout in half and dry as shown in the image. Gently place each set of wings on the folded foil or paper to dry. Once they are dry, create designs on the wings using either edible markers (available at cake and craft supply stores) or a small paintbrush dipped in various food colors mixed with lemon juice. Let dry.

Leaves   When I'm making traditional green leaves, I tend to pipe them out of buttercream with the specialty number-67 tip for a contrast against the more sculpted sugar-paste flowers. This adds more dimension to the cake and gives it a softer, more natural look. When you're making leaves, keep the color on the more olive or acid green side for an unconventional and surprising look. To achieve these colors, use forest-green or leaf-green food coloring, adding bits of lemon yellow and chocolate brown to mellow the brightness.

For cutting the leaf shape out of sugar paste, use a small, sharp knife to create leaves that are irregular—and more true to nature. If you use a cutter, look for an elongated-leaf cutter or a rosebud-leaf cutter. These shapes are not so plump and squat and tend to harmonize nicely with most flowers.

I also suggest that you buy a couple of leaf veiners, too, which are molded silicone leaves with protruding veins. After you cut out a leaf, place it on the veiner and press it lightly with the roller to create realistic veins. I love the look of a rough, hand-cut leaf shape detailed with the veiner—it's like a leaf plucked from a bush.

DRYING SUGAR PASTE

After you rub each petal, let it dry upside down to achieve a beautiful sculpted look. I dry flowers on recycled egg cartons—they are the perfect shape, and depending on which side you use, you can achieve a larger, more open-faced flower or a tighter, closed flower. And because the cartons stack well, they're easy to store.

It's best to use up as much of the colored sugar paste as you make. Even stored in plastic wrap, sugar paste has a tendency to harden with time. If you make extra flowers or shapes, future decorating will be a cinch because you already have them on hand.

The drying time is typically a day. However, if it's humid or you're in a rush, you can use your oven to speed up the process:

Egg cartons are the perfect mold for drying sugar—paste flowers

Preheat the oven to 180°F. Place the sugar-paste petals on paper egg cartons on a baking sheet, and bake for 1/2 hour. Turn off oven and let the flowers cool inside the oven, up to 1 hour. Unfortunately, humidity seems to keep sugar flowers soft, so if you're working on a humid day, let the flowers dry out as long as possible in the oven and decorate the cake close to the serving time.

STORING

Sugar-paste creations can keep for years, and storing them is easy. I recycle the plastic take-out food containers and line them with a paper towel or napkin. Place the flowers on top of the paper towel, and then cover the flowers with another layer of paper towel; repeat, leave enough room so that when you put the top on the container, you do not crush the flowers.

Piped Decorations

Piped decorations are elegant and easy when you don't have the time for sugar-paste decorations, or if you want to make something look fantastic without a lot of effort. My secret—using oversize pastry tips for small cupcakes and cakes—makes a rich, luscious topping that you just want to take a bite out of. Starting at the outer edge of the cupcake, apply steady pressure to the piping bag, moving it in a slow circle around the outer edge and toward the center. When you reach the middle of the cupcake, push down slightly on the center of the piping bag, releasing the pressure.

It's best to order these tips online, where you can see samples of the piping styles. I like clean, plain-edged tips and small-toothed large tips for swirly effects. Be sure to get a matching large coupler and bag, which are different than the standard coupler sizes typically sold for piping cakes.

You can create a range of looks from just a handful of piping tips. I still have my piping kit from a cake-decorating class I took five years ago, and I haven't used even half the tips. The tips I use most are sizes 0, 1, 2, 4, 7, and 12. These are all clean-edged round tips that I use for piping stamens in flowers, writing words, or creating

From top to bottom:
star tip, size 12,
size 10, small star tip,
size 2, size 0

beadwork on the edges. I do like having a leaf number-67 tip on hand for piping leaves, and once in a blue moon, I pipe chrysanthemums, which requires a number-81 tip. Otherwise, I use only the oversize tips and these regular-size tips, and I leave decorations like basketweave, bows, and swags to precision masters.

I prefer buying disposable bags, as the maintenance of coated fabric pastry bags is tedious and requires lots of washing (to eliminate color stains and buttery residue). The plastic bags are easy to use and can be recycled after you rinse them in hot water.

To fill a pastry bag Snip the corner and drop the larger half of the coupler into the bag, with the smaller opening facing the cut corner. Place the metal tip on top, and screw it in place with the smaller plastic ring. Now you're ready to fill your bag.

Roll the outer edge of the pastry bag down about 2 inches, as you would the cuff of a pant except upside down. Hold the bag open and fill it almost to the tip, pushing the frosting into the bag so that there are no air pockets to interfere with your piping. Fill the bag until you have about 4 inches left at the top. Gently pinch the bag right to where the frosting is filled, and twist it twice, keeping the twist closed in your right hand. This hand will apply pressure and push the cream out. Your left hand will guide the bag. (If you're left-handed, switch these directions accordingly.) You can practice piping techniques on parchment paper, a stainless-steel table, or, as shown, an overturned cake board.

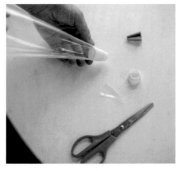

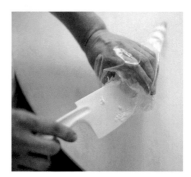

Filling a standard pastry bag. Make sure you twist the top so that frosting doesn't squeeze out all over your hand!

Chocolate Decorations

For her wild 1980s dinner parties, my mom used to melt those pre-fab chocolate disks to make chocolate-covered strawberries. It was all the rage back then, but when I use chocolate to decorate, that taste is something I'd like to leave in the past.

For melting chocolate, you can use either a double boiler or a microwave; however, the double boiler is always a foolproof way to melt chocolate without risking burning or having it "seize."

For dark or milk chocolate, I like making chocolate leaves—a very simple, chic, and tasty way to decorate desserts. All you need to have on hand is your favorite organic chocolate and some clean leaves that have not been sprayed with any pesticides or chemicals, such as lemon or rose leaves. First wash and dry the leaves, and then place them on a parchment-lined baking sheet with the side of the leaf with the more pronounced vein facing up. Melt some chocolate in a double boiler. Using a small metal spatula, spread a thick layer of chocolate, about 1/8 inch thick, on the leaf. Then place the coated leaf in the refrigerator to chill and harden, about 15 minutes. Gently peel the real leaf away from the chocolate. Once all the leaves have been peeled off, place the chocolate leaves back in the refrigerator until you are ready to garnish with them. They melt extremely quickly and are sensitive to heat. If you don't have leaves, you can use silicone veiners as faux leaf molds (see page 232).

Because chocolate is fragile and sensitive to changes in temperature, I usually decorate a fancy pudding with leaves at the last minute, or decorate a cake with chocolate leaves only in the winter, to keep it generally cool.

Metallic Powder Dusting

The cake decorating industry produces colorful and metallic powders or "dusts" for accenting flowers or for painting on cakes. There are three types—petal, luster, and metallic dusts. The powders are all nontoxic, derived from minerals, and can be used as powders or made into a liquid "paint."

Petal dust provides color without shine or shimmer. I use it for matte details, such as dusting the edge of a flower. In my cake decorating class, we used a pale green petal dust on the edge of white roses to give them a natural look.

Luster dust is a shimmery powder that has subtle sparkle. It is not as concentrated as the metallic dust, and comes in a wide range of iridescents as well as colors. It can be dusted lightly on a flower or chilled ganache to give it a shimmer.

Metallic dust has a high shine metallic finish. It is best used for details such as a gold painted stamen in the center of a flower, or gold branches on a cake. My favorite use for metallic dust is to hand-brush it on my Goldies (page 137).

There are several ways to use the dusts. You can dip a paintbrush in them straight from their container, or mix them with a clear alcohol or lemon juice to make a paint. You can mix colors and matte or shimmery dust to create a custom palette or effect. Some fun new products use the dusts in a spray form, such as metallic luster spray, which can cover a batch of cupcakes in a shimmery finish. You can find it at www.cakedeco.com and www.sugarcraft.com.

Hand—Painted Touches

Hand-painting gives a cake an artisanal touch and sets it apart from traditional fancy cakes. I mix metallic or luster dust with clear alcohol to create a paint that I use for vines and branches. You can also use this paint for other details, such as small dots along the cake edges, hand-painted leaves, or small dashes in iridescent dust if you make sugar-paste butterflies—to show them fluttering around!

Decorating a Cake with Vines and Flowers

Chilled frosted cakes make the ideal base for hand-painting or piping vines: Starting at one edge on top of the cake, hand-paint or pipe a branch with the number 0 or 1 tip. Work your way across the cake to create a few branches. These branches will be your guide when placing flowers. I generally like to position the branches and flowers in a diagonal direction, from the top edge to the bottom. This creates a nice visual direction. Also paint a few vines coming up from the bottom of the cake, so that the cake is covered on all sides. When painting with a brush, you may have to adjust how much pigment you add to make your "paint," to make it opaque or more translucent. Be sure not to apply too much pressure when you are painting with the brush, or else it will dig into the frosting.

I like to use an odd number of shapes or flowers to create a dynamic design, as is often done in jewelry design and other art forms as a reference to the harmony of nature. If you're using flowers, start with three or five large flowers. Add smaller flowers around the larger ones. To the left or right diagonally, on the bottom edge of the cake, add another cluster of flowers.

To create depth and texture, place a smaller flower inside a larger one, with a dab of frosting underneath the small flower, pressing slightly to secure it.

I use a dab of frosting to secure the flowers on the cake.

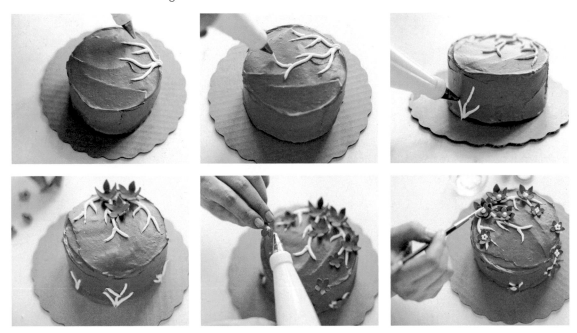

piping and painting the flower stamen   I arrange the flowers and then pipe the centers with frosting or ganache to create the stamens. When piping the stamens, I vary the centers to keep things interesting. To achieve large dots, press the pastry-bag tip close to the center of the flower, squeezing the bag as a large ball of frosting comes out. Release the pressure on the bag and lift it straight up. Any peaks can be smoothed out with a finger dipped in water. You can range the sizes of the dots—three medium dots, four small dots, and so on—just to keep the feeling light and varied.

To paint the centers of the flowers with a metallic finish, use a paintbrush to mix 1/2 teaspoon lemon juice with a pinch of the dust in a bowl. Load the paintbrush with the metallic dust mixture, and gently dab the brush on the stamen to cover the center.

Instead of using a metallic dust, you can use a contrasting frosting color for the stamen. For pink flowers, a pale acid yellow looks

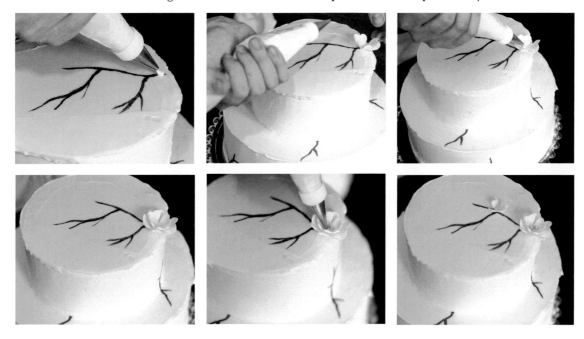

chic; for blue flowers, a pale salmon pink works well; and for choco-late flowers, a light Wedgwood blue looks pretty. Sometimes just tinting one batch of buttercream two different colors is an easy way to give your cake sophistication.

For a daisy or anemone center as seen on the Vanilla-Bean Butter Cake (page 37), pipe a 1/4-inch circle of small dots with a small tip (size 2). I usually select the Melted Chocolate Ganache (page 140) for this, piping a dark outer ring and filling in the center with a colored frosting. Once I've piped the small dots, I use a brush loaded with wet metallic dust to lightly touch the center. The wet dust will cling to the tops of the dots, creating a dimensional look.

TIERING A CAKE

When you make a high layer cake or any tiered cake, you'll need an internal support system so that the cake remains stable, especially while you're frosting, decorating, or transporting it. With sticks inside the cake, you can build layer upon layer and not worry about the weight causing it to topple.

To tier a cake, you will need paper lollipop sticks, available at most craft stores, cake-supply shops, and online. To determine the number of lollipop sticks needed, use the measurement of the top cake and add one. For example, a 4-inch top cake will require five sticks, and a 6-inch top cake will require seven.

Place your frosted cakes on cake rounds (see page 250). Place one stick into the center of the bottom cake. The stick should be sticking out of the top. Place the remaining sticks at 1 1/2 to 2 inches from the center stick, with equal space between them. Slightly raise each stick and use a pencil to mark the spot just below where the stick extended above the cake. Once you mark all the sticks, remove them, cut them at the marks with a sharp knife or scissors, and reinsert the cut sticks into the cake. The tops should be slightly below the top of the cake.

Trim the cake board of the second cake just to the edge of where it has been frosted, so that the board is not visible. This will support the second layer on the tiers. Place the second cake on top of the first, eyeballing to center it. If there is a third tier, repeat the process with the sticks and the cake board.

When you're cutting the cake, take care to remove the sticks from the pieces, or make sure to let the host know so that no one is surprised to find a white stick in their slice of cake!

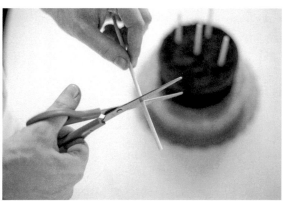

PRESENTATION
CHIC WAYS TO DISPLAY TREATS

Whenever I visit my family in Chicago, I stop at a few thrift stores. There I always find great china cups and a smattering of china plates, usually for a dollar each. I buy several, and when I go to a dinner party or visit family, I bring my cake or dessert on the plate as part of the sweet offering. When you're hosting a dinner party or any kind of gathering, it creates a beautiful table to use an assortment of vintage plates, perhaps with a common motif such as flowers or a few unifying colors. I also like to turn a nice teacup upside down and place a vintage plate, right side up, on top—with a few dabs of epoxy to keep it in place. You always can pull it apart afterward, but the presentation is perfect for serving cookies at a tea party.

Some tips for chic presentation

- Shop thrift stores for random china plates, teacups, and bowls. Use these to present your sweets to guests as part of a housewarming gift.
- Bake fancy cakes with old Jell-O molds, or use them as mini serving dishes for curds.
- Line baskets with vintage tea towels to hold cookies.
- Layer plates for textural presentation. For example, if you have a 7-inch cake, place it on an 8-inch plate of one color, stacked on a 10-inch plate with a different color or print, and then on a glass or ceramic 10-inch cake stand.
- Never underestimate the power of contrasting materials: Wrap a box of cookies or bars in kraft paper and tie it with a metallic bow or a fancy silk ribbon. If you travel abroad, save the local newspaper as wrapping paper; it makes for a very glamorous, international presentation. Or use a bright colored wrapping paper tied with natural twine or sisal.
- I also save heaps of drawings by the kids in a drawer to use as last-minute wrapping paper. It's fun and witty to see their pictures used as part of a homemade gift.

For Ruby's first birthday, I placed cupcakes in vintage child-size china cups.

baking tools

When I first started baking cakes, I would use whatever cake pan happened to be lying around: a giveaway from my roommate's brother, a hand-me-down Bundt pan from a cousin in Chicago, a loaf pan I picked up at the grocery store for a few bucks. Naturally, as I began to bake more, proper pans became necessary, and I found it easy to stock my baking kitchen with pans from cookware stores.

CAKE PANS

It's important to have three round cake pans of the same size, whether 8 or 9 inch, because most cake recipes are created for these sizes. When you're in the mood for a dramatic cake, having three layers means your cake will be higher and more impressive. Basic aluminum cake pans can be purchased for less than $10 each. The smaller (4- or 6-inch) pans are an easy and fun way to make your cakes look more spectacular. Having a variety of sizes on hand will enable you to make tier cakes from one batch of batter. Quite often I will use one batch of batter to fill two 6-inch pans and one 4-inch pan—it's a fancier way to present a birthday cake, and it just looks more important.

BAKING SHEETS

Baking sheets are essential for baking cookies. They can be found at cookware shops or online. Silpats are silicone mats you can place (unbuttered) on top of baking sheets to prevent sticking. If you don't have them, use foil or parchment paper as specified in the recipes.

MIXING BOWLS

Some recipes for cake batters and frostings contain acidic ingredients, such as lemon juice, that can react with the surface of bowls treated with glazes or other corrosible coatings. Plastic bowls tend to harbor grease and other films of dirt that will deflate your egg whites. That's why I only use glass and stainless-steel bowls for mixing and whipping up my sweets. You can easily find a set of three to five bowls that range in size—perfect for organizing your ingredients before you start mixing.

MIXER

When I got engaged, the first thing I registered for was a shiny, fire-engine-red standing KitchenAid mixer. I was so ecstatic the day my mother-in-law purchased it for me—I felt that I didn't even need a wedding anymore, since I finally had the KitchenAid of my dreams! That beautiful piece of machinery still sits in my kitchen almost six years later, working hard for me and making things easy on my arm muscles. If there ever is an investment to be made in the kitchen, this is it. It helps out with everything from beating a batter to kneading dough and whipping whites. Short of cleaning up after itself, it's the greatest baking invention since the oven. Of course, you can make all the recipes in this book with a handheld mixer or even with a whisk, as I did for years. Your arms will be really toned too!

SILICONE SPATULA

I have a few sizes of silicone spatulas on hand for different purposes. Smaller spatulas are great for stirring chocolate in a double boiler, and larger ones are useful for scraping down the sides of the mixing bowl when making frostings or batters.

PARCHMENT PAPER, WAX PAPER, AND BUTTER WRAPPERS

These papers are stealth helpers in the baking kitchen. When you cut them out to fit the bottom of a baking pan, they ensure that your cake will not stick to the bottom. Parchment paper has a higher burning point than wax paper, so use it for baking cakes or cookies. Wax paper is the perfect place to lay cookies that have just been dipped in chocolate.

I feel very eco-savvy when I reuse butter wrappers for the bottom of cake or brownie pans. They make the perfect coating because they're already covered with a thin film of butter. Just fold each one in fours and snip the corner off in a rounded shape and place it in the pan, buttered side up. It will open up into a round that's perfect for smaller pans.

CAKE ROUNDS

Cake rounds are pieces of cardboard that are coated on one side with a grease-resistant white or metallic sheet. They're handy support bases for transporting cakes and essential if you're tiering a cake (page 242). While decorating, I typically use the cake round as the base, and then transfer the cake, with the cake round, onto a cake stand (a cake stand won't always fit in the refrigerator!). Look for cake rounds at any cake-supply store or order them online. They come in a range of sizes; I prefer to use 8- or 9-inch rounds. In a pinch, you can use the bottom of a two-part tart pan.

PASTRY BAG AND TIPS

When I took classes at the Institute of Culinary Education, we had to wash out our pastry bag after each use, and it was such a pain. After a while it was coated with gunk from all the colors that managed to dye it. I started to use clear disposable bags. Although they don't make me feel as fancy, they're a breeze to clean, and because suppliers typically sell them in batches, you can always keep some in reserve.

Although I have a pastry kit with dozens of tips, I find myself using a few basic ones more than others. (See page 235 for instruction on which tips to use and how to use them.) They can be rinsed in hot water and recycled, so you can feel less wasteful about using several pastry bags on one cake!

WHISKS

It's important to own a small and a large whisk—and a few other sizes if you're a serious baker. I prefer a small whisk when I'm melting chocolate in a double boiler and a larger whisk when I'm incorporating many wet ingredients as a step in a recipe. I would avoid any whisk that is gadgetlike or gimmicky; a simple wire whisk always works.

THERMOMETER

A candy thermometer that's made especially for small saucepans and baking needs is essential for making the Marshmallow Frosting (page 88) and will come in handy elsewhere too.

MICROPLANE ZESTER

Conventionally grown citrus fruit is given a wax coating that contains pesticides, herbicides, and other gunk. For this reason, it's really important to use organic or homegrown lemons, oranges, limes, and other citrus fruits.

The thin small blades of a Microplane zester cut spices, such as whole nutmeg, and the peel of fruit into minuscule pieces that are perfect for incorporating into batters and frostings. The zester slices into just the top outermost layer of citrus, so the bitter white pith does not get zested. The tool is really sharp, so be especially careful with kids around. This is definitely an essential for your baking kitchen; you will find Microplanes in kitchenware stores.

MEASURING CUPS AND SPOONS

I prefer stainless-steel measuring cups that stack into one another. Avoid plastic ones, as they are porous and can harbor grease and bacteria. I also own a set of stainless-steel measuring spoons, but my favorite are the sliding measuring spoons called "Pro Measuring Spoon" that make your measuring a one-stop process. I keep two sets: one set for wet ingredients and the other for dry. They're available at stores where baking supplies are sold.

Using Your Oven

Even if you dutifully set your oven to 350°F, varying factors can push the temperature higher or lower. You'll want to build a relationship with your oven and learn its habits and tendencies, as this is the true way to know if your baked goods are done. An oven thermometer will let you know if the thermostar is accurate.

When you're baking, be sure to monitor the oven toward the end. *Never* open the over door while something is in the middle of baking, as it will allow cool air in and deflate your cake or cupcakes. Try to judge the doneness with the oven light or by the baking time.

TOOLS FOR MELTING CHOCOLATE: DOUBLE BOILER OR MICROWAVE

I resisted buying a microwave until my son was born, when I soon came to understand the beauty of it when trying to multitask cooking dinners and baking at the same time! While I used to use only a double boiler for most chocolate melting, it can be done in the microwave just as efficiently—but with a little more attention. If you don't have a double boiler, you can create your own by placing a glass or stainless-steel bowl on top of a small saucepan that is filled with a few inches of simmering water; the indirect heat will slowly melt the chocolate in the bowl. With the microwave, you place the chocolate in a microwave-safe bowl and heat it on full power in small intervals (20 to 30 seconds), stirring and checking to ensure that the chocolate doesn't overheat. If you're in a rush or distracted, I would recommend the double boiler as there's less of a chance of overheating the chocolate. Whatever method you choose, you want to remove the chocolate from the heat source as soon as most of it has melted and only a few lumps remain. The residual heat will melt the rest of the chocolate without overheating it. There's nothing sadder than burning fancy organic chocolate when it's late at night and all the grocery stores have closed!

JUICER

A juicer is great for baking, as many recipes call for lemon, lime, or orange juice. It's also useful for other types of dishes. You can use a hand juicer, but sometimes it squirts all over the place and you lose precious juice. I recommend an electric juicer, but a juice press will work with some manual labor.

baking resources

When I'm in a bind and need something right away, I visit my local cake-supply store. Otherwise, I prefer to order online for better values and variety.

Here is a list of my favorite sources for all your baking needs.

Beryl's Cake Decorating & Pastry Supplies   This company carries a huge assortment of cake and decorating supplies, and a good variety of certified kosher products. www.beryls.com

Bridge Kitchenware   A resource for kitchen equipment, especially pans, and other baking supplies. www.bridgekitchenware.com

Broadway Panhandler   A great store in Manhattan that carries a variety of baking supplies and kitchen supplies, along with pretty cake stands and ceramics from Europe. www.broadwaypanhandler.com

Kerekes Bakery and Restaurant Equipment   This Brooklyn-based company has great prices on larger quantities of items, such as pastry bags, cake boards, and candles. www.bakedeco.com

Michaels   A fantastic chain of craft stores with baking supplies, ribbons, decorations, packaging ideas, etc. www.michaels.com

New York Cake & Baking Distributors   A New York City shop that carries cake boards, food colors, and most of the supplies you will need.

56 West 22nd Street
New York, NY 10010
(212) 675-2253

Pfeil and Holing, Inc.   A resource for cake supplies that I use for buying large quantities of cake boards, metallic dusts, tips, bags, and éclair wrappers. They're friendly and offer great deals when you buy in larger volumes. The store is in Queens, New York. www.cakedeco.com

Sugarcraft   This resource has a great section on cookie cutters, fun new products, and instructional books. It's my favorite site for checking out what is new in the cake world and for finding new ideas for making things. www.sugarcraft.com

Williams—Sonoma, Crate & Barrel, Sur La Table, Target   These stores carry simple baking supplies such as pans, baking sheets, measuring cups, bowls, zesters, mixers, spatulas, whisks, etc. They don't specialize in cake decorating, but they will cover your basic needs.

    www.williams-sonoma.com

    www.crateandbarrel.com

    www.surlatable.com

    www.target.com

Wilton Products, Inc.   Their Web site offers some simple instructional pictures and information explaining cake decorating. Their style, while traditional and tame, is well executed. www.wilton.com

resources for information: organic foods and nutrition

I like to support companies that not only provide quality organic ingredients but also support a greater environmental philosophy—helping the environment and communities surrounding them. As a natural extension of this philosophy, the products these companies create go beyond just attaining USDA certification. Here is a list of my favorite organic resources.

Environmental Working Group
1436 U Street NW, Suite 100
Washington, DC 20009
(202) 667-6982
www.ewg.org
www.foodnews.org

Their easy-to-use Web sites rank produce by levels of contamination, provide information about pesticides in your pet food and meat, and much more.

O'Mama Report
www.theorganicreport.com

This Web site provides updated information about recent studies on organic foods, as well as some interesting articles about pesticides and children and the benefits to new mothers of eating organic. I love checking on the site once in a while, particularly for articles from Europe regarding advances in organic food and technology.

Organic Farming Research Foundation (OFRF)
PO Box 440
Santa Cruz, CA 95061
www.ofrf.org

This Web site offers information about organic farming: how to support it and how to learn more about it.

Organic Trade Association (OTA)
PO Box 547
Greenfield, MA 01302
www.ota.com

This great Web site is filled with information regarding "going organic" and provides links to other sites that discuss farming techniques, new research, and other up-to-date information.

Organic Valley Family of Farms
www.organicvalley.coop

This Web site provides a wealth of information about organic dairy and other foods. When the farmers' market is not around, I buy their whole milk. (Their cows are very happy!)

Quality Assurance International (QAI)
9191 Towne Centre Drive, Suite 510
San Diego, CA, 92122
www.qai-inc.com

This third-party inspection agency verifies organic products and origins. Look for their seal on some organic products.

Rodale Institute
611 Siegfriedale Road
Kutztown, PA 19530-9320
www.rodaleinst.org

This Pennsylvania farm is known for its Farming Systems Trial (FST), the longest-running U.S. experiment specifically designed to compare organic and conventional farming practices. Their Web site includes research and interesting information, as well as directions to their farm.

USDA
www.ams.usda.gov/nop/

The cut-and-dried information for organic legislation and guidelines. According to the USDA, "organic food is produced without using most conventional pesticides, bioengineering, synthetic fertilizers, or ionizing radiation."

The Weston A. Price Foundation
www.westonaprice.org/index.html

Nutrition pioneer Weston A. Price's legacy of nutrition and healthful eating is detailed on this Web site. One of his followers, Sally Fallon, has written a fantastic book called *Nourishing Traditions,* which details ways to improve your diet by sprouting grains, through enzyme enrichment, and with other healthy ideas.

acknowledgments

Infinite gratitude to my husband, Johnny Dwyer, my true love and late-night baking crisis adviser. Thanks for supporting my dreams, even if our house is covered under an eternal blanket of flour.

Thank you to Clyde and Ruby for opening my eyes to what is truly important in the world. Our kitchen dance parties make life worth living.

Thanks to my brother, David Magid, and my sister, Lizzy Ross, for your love and all the years of fun in the kitchen, laughing uncontrollably every time we get together.

To my dad, Zalman. I love you so much, and thanks for all your support and bad jokes. Along with my stepmom, Elizabeth, I know you would love each bite even with freezer burn!

Kim Ficaro, you see beauty like no other. Thank you for devoting so much time to make magic happen, and for all your support, friendship, pure genius, and love.

To Noah Sheldon, thank you for your gorgeous photographs and years of friendship.

To Quinn Latimer, thank you for your help editing my craziness from the early stages.

Thanks to the VIP Cookbook Club—Alicia Humphries, Kolt Beringer, Gary Johnson, Min-Young Lim, Colombe Derstine-Jacobsen, Paige Prather, Freyja Gallagher, Melissa McDonnell, and Matthew Congdon—for your love of food, your exquisite taste buds, and your baking help. May we eat sweets until we drop dead from diabetes.

A special shout-out to Karyn Starr Johnson; thank you for coming to the rescue so many times during the making of this book.

Thank you to my friends and family, whom I love so much and thank: Elizabeth Gilchrist, Daniel Ahearn and Amy Kehoe-Ahearn, Gina Zimmerman, James Wilson, Amy Fulford, Presston Brown, Todd Nickey, Jeanne and Jackson McLaughlin, Amy and Erin Steinhauser, Sara McSweeny, the entire Dwyer family, Ari and Sarah Maizel, Maggie Peng, Peter Kline, Beefcake, Mike O'Connell, Carolyn and Kai Krienke, and Carter and Amanda Little.

To my limited friends, Denise Venice, Daphna Hoffman, Lilia Levin, and Min Young-Lim, thanks for supporting me!

Thanks to Nicolette Camille Florals and Lesley Unruh for their beauty at Ruby's first birthday party.

To my literary agent, Carla Glasser, thank you for your humor and wonderful advice.

I am grateful to the wonderful group at Harper-Collins: David Sweeney, Cassie Jones, Johnathan Wilber, and Maggie Sivon. And a special thanks to Michael Barrs, who picked up my cake downstairs and triggered the events that led to this book being born.

Finally, thanks to Jan & Aya in Greenpoint, Brooklyn, for allowing me to shoot in their beautiful space, and to Sapua in Red Hook, Brooklyn, for allowing me to shoot the cover photo in their inspiring store.

index

Note: *Italicized* page numbers indicate photographs.